Don't Bypass Red Flags

Jessica Lewis

JOA Press
Seminole, Florida

Contents

Part III

Hope Even in the Unknown

This book is dedicated to all those who have endured great heartache loving someone who is a drug addict. May this book help you heal, feel and become empowered, know that you are not alone, and most importantly, invite God into the driver's seat in your life.

I also want to dedicate this book to my ex-husband. Thank you for this major life lesson. I continue to pray you will allow God to heal you and that you begin to live the life He has intended for you to live, drug free. If and when you surrender, I'll be the one clapping the loudest for your achievement.

Introduction

As I stood at the altar, ready to embark on a lifelong journey with the love of my life, I believed I was stepping into my happily ever after. Little did I know that a few months into our marriage, a veil other than the bridal one would be lifted, revealing my husband's hidden double life—fraught with lies, drugs, and an unfathomable betrayal. The boundaries between his secret world and our shared reality blurred, laying bare the harsh truths about his lifestyle and priorities.

Upon reaching the age of thirty, much of my life had unfolded according to plan. I had reached significant milestones, entered into marriage, and was expecting a child. On the surface, it seemed I was living my dream life. However, the reality beneath the façade began to surface. I became aware of the secret lifestyle my husband was entangled in—a life he actively concealed from me. It was a lifestyle I had vehemently avoided since my adolescence: drug addiction—a path I wanted no part of.

My narrative is all too familiar, a tale woven into the fabric of countless lives. Many of us find ourselves entwined with loved ones grappling with drug addiction, bearing burdens in the hope that they might undergo a transformative epiphany and relinquish their destructive lifestyle. Wrestling with questions and self-doubt becomes a consuming part of our journey, as we grapple with the aftermath of dealing with someone ensnared by drug abuse. How did this happen? Why were the red flags not apparent? What alternative actions could I have taken? Did my love fall short? Did I unknowingly contribute to their descent into drugs? Is this somehow my fault? While the answers may seem evident to others, they remain obscured for those entangled in such situations, intricately tied to the tumultuous landscape of our emotions.

For those who've walked in my footsteps, it's crucial to understand that you are not accountable for the decisions your loved ones made. They were individuals grappling with their own wounds, resorting to misguided coping mechanisms to navigate circumstances they couldn't confront directly. I struggled with embracing this truth for a considerable period, but there is genuine validity here. Those caught in the throes of drug abuse often harbor underlying issues they struggle to address. It becomes their responsibility to confront these problems and willingly seek help for any meaningful change to transpire.

If you have suspicions of a loved one being a drug abuser, my aim in this book is to assist you in recognizing the telltale signs and discerning when it's crucial to step back and assess your situation thoroughly. Hence, my intention is to illuminate these indicators and offer clarity to help you see your circumstances more objectively. What exactly do I mean by red flags? They are signals pointing to unhealthy behaviors or traits that may pose harm to both you and others. Red flags act as warning signs, indicating that something may be off.

I will also discuss the most challenging aspect—learning to release. Letting go is imperative for safeguarding your well-being and maintaining sanity amid the turmoil caused by drug abuse. Tough love, though incomprehensible to a drug user in the moment, stands as one of the most profound expressions of love. While it may not resonate with them immediately, when they eventually emerge from the haze, they will recognize that receiving tough love was pivotal for reaching rock bottom and paving the way for a transformative journey toward a drug-free, improved life.

Don't Bypass Red Flags chronicles my journey with my former husband, offering insights gained from the aftermath to empower those facing similar circumstances. Within these pages, I've compiled a concise catalog of red flags that I, regrettably, overlooked for an extended period. By openly sharing these signals and the wisdom acquired once I acknowledged them, my aim is to assist others in swiftly recognizing such indicators in their own lives. I battled against my own better judgment for an extended period in the name of love. I aspire to guide others toward the understanding that the most profound way to express love is by heeding one's better judgment. Your intuition exists for a reason, and in the midst of a relationship with a drug addict, they may manipulate your sense of right and wrong. Don't allow their mind games to sway you. Trust your instincts, and if you find yourself adrift, seek wisdom through prayer.

"If any of you lacks wisdom, you should ask God, who gives generously to all without finding fault, and it will be given to you." James 1:5 (NIV)

Part I

Identifying Red Flags

Chapter One

Fairy Tale Lies

Sometimes life just knocks you off your feet and you're floating on air. That's exactly what happened when Brent came into my life. He embodied everything I ever wished for in a man—handsome, charming, and shared my values. His eyes were the perfect shade of blue, and his dimples and smile drew you in. I admired the way he carried himself—a humble man who admitted to his past failures and made strides to never repeat his mistakes. Our love story unfolded quickly and intensely.

Brent and I had attended middle school together and shared some of the same friends. However, back then, we only exchanged simple hellos or waves in the hallways. In high school and college, our paths diverged, only to cross again a few years after I finished school, thanks to social media. To be quite honest, Brent wasn't my type when we were younger, but after seeing his "glow up" as an adult, I was intrigued. Liking pictures turned into commenting on pictures. It eventually led to swapping numbers and meeting in person. From there, we became inseparable.

Our first few years together were wonderful—dating, traveling, surprising one another with gifts, and simply enjoying each other's company. It was pure bliss. Soon, we got engaged. His proposal marked the first time he brought tears to my eyes. We were secluded in the Caribbean on a cruise, and he poured his heart out, expressing love and excitement over calling me his wife. He wiped away every tear of joy and planted a sweet kiss on my forehead. I was floating on air. As far as I was concerned, I was the luckiest woman alive to have a man who I thought was everything on my checklist, ask for my hand in marriage. I could not wait to share our wonderful news once we returned home, but more importantly to share his last name.

I later discovered that he had taken the time to meet with my father and brother, seeking their approval before proposing to me. On the same day, he went to my mother, expressed his sincere apologies for approaching my brother first, and sought her blessing. Additionally, he called my sister, who lived out of state, and asked her as well. How blessed was I to have someone so considerate? While it's common for a groom to ask for the bride's father's blessing as a sign of respect, involving the entire family was unique and special. I had not heard of this happening to anyone I knew. Being in love with a man who demonstrated such consideration convinced me that he was truly the perfect match for me. He was the one.

There was not a day that went by when I didn't look at him and not wrap my arms around him. I was madly in love and made sure he and everyone in my world knew it. This man came into my life when I least expected it and added so much value. This was how fairy tale romances began—the ones that were supposed to last a lifetime. I could not see a future that did not include him. He meant more to me than I could put into words, and I looked forward to permanently merging our lives. Looking back, all my dreams of marriage, having a wedding, and creating and raising a family were finally going to be a reality.

Two weeks after we were engaged, on a late Friday afternoon, I received a phone call from a friend. Her voice was filled with worry when she asked where I was. Confused, I told her I was at home. Then she asked if I knew where my fiancé was. As soon as I asked why, she said, "Okay, I'm on the turnpike and I drove past an accident, and I believe I saw him on the side of the road. His SUV is green, right?" I remember her telling me exactly where the accident was and that he appeared to be all right. Without hesitation, I drove to the scene. I called him numerous times before finally getting a response while I was stopped at a gas station. He said he was getting arrested. My mind raced, and I recall screaming and asking him how he could answer the phone if he was getting arrested.

Once I arrived at the accident, I saw my fiancé in handcuffs sitting on the median facing the opposite side of traffic. A state trooper stood alongside him, and a tow truck had his totaled SUV on the ramp. The traffic moved slowly as everyone was taking turns observing the scene. I watched in disbelief as the officers walked my fiancé over to the back of the police car and put him inside.

The officer approached me and asked who I was to Brent and if I knew he was a convicted felon. He was angry and briefed me on his interaction with my fiancé, "He flat out lied to me and said the gun wasn't his. I'm taking him in." A million thoughts rushed through my head. *What gun? He doesn't have a gun. What does a gun have to do with his car being totaled? How did this accident happen and again, what gun?*

Brent was honest with me about being a convicted felon. Within the first five minutes of our first date, he disclosed his criminal record. He didn't have to tell me. I respected that he was being transparent. Everyone has made mistakes and as long as he owned up to them and did not repeat them, I was in no position to judge. As far as I was aware, Brent did not lie to me about anything...unless he had a surprise planned out for me.

I followed the state trooper to the jail and parked in the parking lot. Once

Brent's mother arrived, I lowered my window. "Is this really happening," I asked and cried. The words that came out of her mouth left me dumbfounded.

"Oh honey, we still have time to return your ring."

I cried even harder. What I should have been thinking was, *what does she know that I don't know that made her say that?* That was the million-dollar question I neglected to ask.

This is where I should have taken a step back and assessed my relationship. A serious red flag was being overlooked—presumably the most important red flag to end this relationship before the many red flags that followed. I was too caught up in my feelings during this time to think with a sound mind—blinded by love. When something confusing happens and we're deeply in love, we may not think logically. Instead, we let our emotions guide us, even if it means not seeing the obvious. We are reminded in Jeremiah 17:9 that the heart is deceitful above all things, so this is where I should have stopped to ask for wisdom. However, this was also a moment that played a pivotal role in shaping the wisdom I have now.

Red Flag # 1: Hiding Something Harmful

When you are dealing with a drug abuser, they will often hide parts of their life from you that are harmful to them, you, and your family. When what they hid eventually comes to light, you feel disoriented, and it can be hard to reconcile the truth of the situation with the reality you've known for so long. This is a signal to pause and reevaluate.

Late that night, after I had bonded Brent out and we went home, I burst into tears yet again. He held me and cried with me. I asked him, "Baby, whose gun was that? Why was there a loaded gun in the car and how did this accident happen?"

"It's one of my old guns, and I was going to give it to a friend to get rid of it because I know you don't like them. The accident happened because some car hit me from the side trying to merge into my lane, pushed me into the guardrail, and the truck flipped over."

I continued with my questions, wanting to know more. Why did he even have a gun, knowing he is a convicted felon and not allowed to possess one? Which friend was he going to see? Why couldn't they come to him? I must have sounded like a broken record because the questions just kept coming and some were repetitive. I focused more on asking questions than taking the time to listen to the answers in detail. Had I redirected my attention to his answers, I could have better dissected his story. The simple truth was that he was lying and doing his best to cover up the fact that he should not have had a gun in his possession. The truth was that there was more than just a gun being hidden. The truth was that more was going to unravel from this, and I would be in for the most chaotic ride of my life.

But I desperately wanted to go back to the reality I was used to; the one where Brent didn't lie to me. I could have made the wise decision to hit the abort button before all the real turmoil unfolded. But I was in love and newly engaged. I genuinely believed this was just a hard time we were going to face together to prove we could overcome anything. Many couples experienced a rough patch during their engagement, and I figured this was ours.

In the months that followed, we committed to moving forward with our wedding plans. Like many couples discover, the wedding preparations were stressful, but we cherished the memories that came with it. Brent always had his court case in the back of his mind, and I did too. However, I opted not to dwell on it, actively reassuring him that we would persevere. I viewed it as a temporary hardship from which we would bounce back. We had God on our side, and everything was going to work out.

As we closed in on Brent's court date, we found that the state attorney did not want to back down from a two-year prison deal. Brent was losing faith and I kept reminding him that we were destined to get married. He was supposed to turn himself in three days after my birthday. I was in complete denial, kept on preaching faith, and continued with the wedding plans which were six months away at that point. My birthday came, and I spent the latter half of it sobbing because of his case. Our lawyer had not heard from the state attorney to see if he could work out another deal. Brent was a bit withdrawn and told me it would be best if we called the wedding off because he was certain he was going to prison. I did not want to believe it. I told him, "I just know we are to be married and you need to trust God. If you love me, you will keep fighting and believe that a miracle is going to happen." I believed it and he didn't. That night was the first night we went to bed on separate pages.

The following morning, I put on a full face of makeup and tried to conceal my sorrow. My head was clouded with thoughts of having to face the possibility that my love may have to surrender himself in less than forty-eight hours. I was heartbroken but still had faith that a miracle would happen. Brent called me mid-afternoon. My heart was racing. I answered with a soft hello. His voice was loud and piercing. "Babe! I just got off the phone with my lawyer; he worked out a five-year probation deal instead of two years in prison! We're getting married!"

I fell to the ground, crying. "I told you!" I repeatedly said, between sobs. The wedding was officially going to happen, and the rest of the planning was filled with more joy and less worry.

Leading up to our wedding day, I couldn't sleep. I kept thinking about our relationship, from our first date to our first kiss, those late-night food runs, the first time we said "I love you," the nights we rushed home to talk for hours, and the tough times after his arrest.

On the eve of our wedding, I found myself fully awake at 4:00 in the morning. I decided to call him, and he answered right away. Turns out, he was having trouble sleeping too, and had thought about calling me. We chatted for less than fifteen minutes, expressing how excited and grateful we were to have come this far. Our conversation was full of love and promises to support each other, grow together, and have faith that we could handle any challenges. Neither of us wanted to hang up, but when we finally did, we were able to drift off to sleep, feeling content.

Our November wedding was immaculate. Every detail I had envisioned in my head was laid out for all those in attendance to see. The fall colors, the lit candles inside of the lanterns, the hints of gold, and the essence of romance all around truly displayed the fairy tale we were living. Hand in hand, we stood smiling and soaking in every moment.

Little did I know, marriage was going to magnify all the issues I thought were just a part of the past. All those "hardships" I thought were a test of love, were warning signs I was completely gullible to. The door that kept all the hidden secrets behind it began to unhinge just months after saying "I do." My life was about to turn upside down and the world I would be exposed to was one I wasn't ready for and didn't want any part of.

We all have secrets, things we don't really want to share with other people. So, when is hiding something a red flag? It becomes a red flag when you sense the person in your life has secrets or when it is revealed they are hiding something that may be harmful to them, you, and your family.

Back then, there were things I didn't realize, but having gone through it, I want to offer you some insights that might be helpful. When you come across the warning signs of a loved one concealing something harmful from you—whether it's a weapon, illegal substances, or a friendship with someone who's a bad influence—know that if they're hiding one thing, there's a good chance there's more they're not telling you.

When drug abusers offer excuses and lie in response to your questions, it is tempting to take them at their word, because you love them and genuinely want to believe them. In these moments, try to focus more on their answers than on your feelings and desires.

Sometimes what we *want* starts trumping and distorting what is *true*. Try to take a few steps back when you find out a loved one is hiding something harmful from you. It can be hard to look past the emotions, the memories, the closeness, and their good characteristics, but you need to see the situation as clearly as possible. That doesn't mean you need to walk away from the person completely; it just means that by taking a few steps back you'll be able to think more clearly about what the next steps should be in your relationship. This will put you in a better position when more secrets inevitably come to light.

It can be hard to learn someone you love has hidden something big from you. It will make you question everything. It may feel like your world has turned upside down. But even in the chaos, God is there, and Hebrews 13:8 (NIV) tells us, "Jesus Christ is the same yesterday and today and forever."

We can go to Him with all our troubles and trust Him to be the rock we can cling to when everything else feels unsteady and uncertain. People change, people make mistakes, people betray us. But God does not change. He is perfect and He cares deeply for us. When we are certain of

God's steadiness, it is easier for us to navigate the confusing new reality we stepped into.

Chapter Two

Circle of Friends

We are direct reflections of the company we keep. Motivational speaker Jim Rohn famously said that we are the average of the five people we spend the most time with.[1] That means the people we hang out with influence our character and impact our decisions. We might believe we can resist adopting the traits of negative influences, but it's akin to working in a bakery while attempting to adhere to a diet. Yes, it's possible, but it sure isn't easy.

Five months into our marriage, my husband would have a poker night with his buddies every weekend. Brent and I had discussed him having friends over, but I was adamant about everyone leaving at a respectable time. I was not too fond of most of the people he brought over. There were two guys, in particular, I would have preferred my husband not associate with at all. I had suspicions one was a drug user and the other a drug dealer. I did bring this matter to Brent's attention; however, he always tried to assure me they were good people and that I should stop being so judgmental. I dropped the subject for some time until one night I came home from working a sixteen-hour shift and lost my cool. I expected our home to be clean and free of company as we discussed over the phone during my lunch break. All I wanted was to take a hot shower, spend time with my husband, and go to sleep before another long day at work. Upon hearing the cards and poker chips tossed onto the table from outside the front door, I stormed inside, yelled at Brent, and told everyone to leave immediately.

Then my lecture began. He was apologetic, cleaned their mess, and said moving forward if he were to have a poker night, it would take place outside. I was reluctant to agree, but I did because I wanted to end the argument. He should have time with his friends, I just wished he had different friends.

A few months later, I went to the living room to have a conversation with Brent. He was in the next room, and we were discussing going out on a sporadic date that night. Suddenly, my eyes shifted to the center of the coffee table. "Brent, what is that?" I tried to rationalize what I was seeing: a large bag with white powder in it. He rushed into the living room with his mouth hanging open. "That's Carl's."

"This is exactly what I think it is, isn't it?" I asked sternly.

"Yes. He left it here the other night and made plans to come by later today to pick it up."

I was infuriated. "I don't care what plans he made with you to come and get it, but I do know that I don't want this crap or him in our house ever again! I told you I didn't like him! You need to cut him off!"

I grabbed the bag of cocaine and forcefully stomped my way to the bathroom. I had every intention of flushing it down the toilet. Brent stopped me before I could open the bag. "Baby, you don't want to open it and get it everywhere or on you. Please, just stop and let me wrap it in another bag. I told him he could come and get it."

I know I said a lot at that moment and most of it was foul language. I was upset and I had every right to be. Why would anyone willingly spend time with people who use cocaine? And more importantly, who allows that kind of stuff in their home and even lets their friends come to pick it up after it's been left behind? That was a red flag moment!

Carl came to pick up his bag of cocaine and apologized to me. I didn't have anything nice to say and after he left, I told Brent that Carl was a friend he would have to cut off for our marriage to work. I was in no mood to negotiate and was triggered when Brent continued to give me excuses. "I've known him since I was seven years old. I don't ask you to cut off any of your friends, and I don't think it's fair for you to ask me to cut off my oldest friend." My head was spinning in circles at this point. I could not understand why it was so important to keep this friendship when there was an apparent lack of respect. You have to respect your spouse enough to recognize when there is a legitimate issue that needs to be addressed. That's the time to honor your marriage and act on the situation accordingly. This was undoubtedly a moment when I should have realized that the problem wasn't solely with Carl, but primarily with my husband.

Red Flag #2: Keeping Bad Company

The company we keep says a lot about us. The people we surround ourselves with will impact our behavior, actions, words, and character. If your loved one is spending time with drug users and/or drug dealers, then they are constantly surrounding themselves with temptation and it is only a matter of time before they give in. When your loved one starts making excuses for and defending their drug abusing and drug dealing friends, refusing to cut them out of their lives, there is likely something else they are unwilling to give up too.

About two weeks later, Brent had another poker night. This time, everyone was outside, drinking and laughing. And the two friends I didn't care for showed up. I was thankful they were all outside, but I was still annoyed they were over in the first place. As time passed, everyone became louder. I started to smell smoke inside, and their trips to the bathroom became frequent. I was furious. Brent had come inside, and I spoke to him in the kitchen. "You've had your fun. They need to go. I would like to enjoy a weekend off without company."

Intoxicated, he responded, "You agreed I could have my friends over if I hosted outside. It's not fair. You get like this every time they're here. I'll just tell them to pee outside, so no one comes in and bothers you anymore." He turned and walked back outside. I had no other words to exchange with him. I followed behind him and locked the door. I figured I was going to enjoy the rest of my night unbothered and when he was ready to come inside, he would knock loud enough for me to let him in. I knew it was petty, but he pushed my buttons, and that's exactly what he ended up doing to come back inside.

The next morning, I woke up and found Brent passed out on the couch. I made breakfast, and when I went to take out the trash, I got another surprise. All their bottles and trash were piled up right in front of our door for everyone passing by to see. Once again, I was furious. I was expecting my cousin Alyssa to come by for our workout, and I was angry and embarrassed. I tried to wake Brent up so he could clean up the mess, but it took a while before he responded. When he finally woke up, he was still drunk. I told him he needed to clean up the mess outside before Alyssa arrived. We argued back and forth, and then he got defensive, grabbed his phone, and started talking on it. I stood there, waiting to hear the other person's voice, with my eyebrow raised.

"I'll be right there," he said.

"Where are you going?" I demanded.

"I have to meet with my probation officer." He attempted to grab the car keys, but I snatched them from the hook before he could get them. Brent ran out the door.

"You're not allowed to be drunk and you're going to their office like that? Come back and give me your phone!" I yelled. He was already down the sidewalk. I wasn't going to chase him and if he got in trouble, so be it. I turned and went back inside.

Of course, he was lying. His appointments with his probation officer were set for Tuesday mornings before he went to work. It was Saturday and their office was closed on the weekend. The only time they would come around on the weekend would be to see if he was home.

Moments later, I heard a knock on the door. It was Alyssa. When I opened the door, she asked what happened as she pointed to the chaos surrounding her. I told her Brent had a poker night and he and his friends left the mess. She and I inspected it together. There were bottles everywhere, the guts from inside Black and Mild cigars piled up, stems from marijuana, and a few small plastic bags. She picked one up and said, "This had cocaine in it. Look, there's white powder left over."

A surge of rage coursed through me. I picked up my phone and called Brent nonstop until I heard, "Hey Jess." I turned around to face the familiar voice and saw it was one of Brent's friends, Ricky. This was not one of the friends that participated in the poker nights. This was a friend I wished Brent would spend more time with.

"What happened here?" he asked.

"Brent had a poker night, and this is the result of it. I'm so over his foolishness and the people he hangs around!" Ricky stood in disbelief and agreed with me that this was out of hand. Ricky asked for a broom and garbage bag so he could clean the mess while I went inside and tried to contact Brent. I called once more and then my phone rang. It was my other cousin Crystal.

"Jess, Brent's here," said Crystal.

Immediately I turned to Ricky and Alyssa and told them I needed to leave. Ricky put the broom away and took the trash out for me. Alyssa asked me to call her later. Within ten minutes, I was at Crystal's house. I quickly discovered that Brent, my cousin Crystal, and her husband Mason all did cocaine. My head ran wild with questions. *How did I not piece this together sooner? Who started who on cocaine? How could I have possibly been this busy and blind to not see this? I can bet anything that the large bag of cocaine I found on the coffee table was indeed Brent's. No wonder he didn't want to stop being friends with Carl because he does drugs with him!*

As the conversation intensified, Brent grew in frustration and pulled a gun from his waistline. There were screams from Crystal, Mason, and myself. My instincts took over as I grabbed Brent's wrist with one hand and smacked the gun out of his grasp with my other hand.

"Get out! It's time for y'all to go," said Mason.

I steered Brent towards the door and Crystal handed me the gun she picked up from the floor.

I got Brent into my car and the drive home was filled with yelling and screaming. Neither of us was listening to the other. I told Brent he had a problem, and that he was going to need to go to rehab to correct it. As I parked, Brent continued to yell and stand firm in his belief that I was overreacting. "Give me back my gun!" he demanded as he reached over me trying to get to the driver's side door.

"No! Just stop!" We wrestled for possession of the gun until Brent overpowered me and took hold of it.

He got out of the car, slammed the door, and headed inside. I called his mom. "Daphne! He's doing cocaine!" I exclaimed.

"I knew it!" She responded.

I asked her to please come over, so we could talk. I hung up the phone feeling confused and once I went inside, found Brent passed out on the couch again. I watched him and cried. Once again, many thoughts ran through my head. *What did she mean she knew it, and why was I not informed of any of her suspicions? Why do mothers like to cover for their sons when they know there's an underlying issue that can potentially cause harm to their family? Why am I the last to know? Was he always like this and now he's gotten sloppy, and his secrets are being exposed? Is this something that started because of the people he has surrounded himself with?* What I should have done was call on God and not Daphne! God should always be our first response and never our last resort!

Once my mother-in-law arrived, I told her everything that had happened. She genuinely appeared concerned. We woke Brent and attempted to have a conversation. I learned that his father had issues with cocaine before Brent was born and addiction ran in the family. Pieces of the puzzle began to assemble in front of me. After she left, I sat on the couch next to Brent as he slept and cried until I eventually fell asleep.

When I woke, Brent was at my feet in tears. "Hey, baby." He said in a soft voice, "I messed up. I know you're mad at me and you have every right to be. I'm so sorry. I love you so much and I want to fix this." We talked for hours. I learned the "truth" about his involvement with cocaine, his friends, and my cousin and her husband's usage. I was upset and felt like such a fool.

"All this time everyone knows the truth about my husband except for me," I told him. "Apparently, I'm lying next to a complete stranger every night. Is this who I really married? Is this really you? Huh? Cause you got exactly who you thought you married. I don't have any secrets of any kind from you!"

He sat beside me motionless and nodded in agreement. After our lengthy discussion, we finally came to a resolution. We agreed to be honest with each other no matter what. No more secrets. He vowed to stop hanging with those friends—including my cousin and her husband. We went to church and prayed together often. If he felt he was stressed and wanted to drink or use any substance, he would come to me, and we would seek help together.

According to Brent, he wasn't in too deep and that was the biggest lie I believed. Somehow, he managed to convince me to think it was something he did only once in a blue moon. How this man was capable of getting me to go against my intuition is beyond me. There were countless times I felt in my gut something was off; each time I felt I was overanalyzing the situation, but in actuality, I was on the right track. In that moment, I once again suppressed my better judgment and chose to believe in him. That conversation we had was a turning point in our relationship. His poker night friends were not coming around, he was more open with me, we discussed God and our faith, and anytime he felt stressed he spoke to me about it. Things were looking up and I was proud of the changes he had made. When this became our norm, I thought back to my doubts and concluded I was overthinking. He did make changes and I was happy with them.

By the time the new year came around, Brent and I were happy, content, and madly in love. We rang in the new year with a bonfire and wrapped in each other's arms. I tired soon after the ball dropped, so we went home. The following days I had no energy and finally, we had suspicions that I might be pregnant. I took a test and sure enough, I was. We were overjoyed, shared our plans of being the best parents to our son or daughter, and fell asleep holding my stomach. This was our new beginning. We were ecstatic. On the surface, Brent made necessary changes, our relationship was flourishing, and we had a bundle of joy to look forward to, come September. Life appeared to be going in the direction we planned but the manipulation he had rolled up his sleeve would soon unfurl.

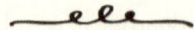

Even though I noticed some behavioral changes in Brent, he was still unwilling to let go of some friendships that were bad for him and didn't serve him. This was a red flag that I stared straight at for a while, hoping against my better judgment that Brent was being honest with me. 1 Corinthians 15:33 (NIV) says, "Do not be misled: Bad company corrupts good character." Bad company corrupts. Period. We imitate those who we surround ourselves with. And if you are surrounded by people who are negative influences whether through their words or actions, you will begin to imitate them. The opposite is true as well. If you surround yourself with people who are positive and uplifting, they will rub off on you and your words and actions will be positively impacted.

When you are around people who are honest and speak truth, your life will be filled with truth. When you are around people who make you question yourself and who regularly lie, your life will be full of lies and you will always be questioning yourself. Carefully look at your circle of friends and the circle of friends your loved one spends time with. If there are any bad influences in your circle, consider removing them and finding people who share your values and goals. If your loved one is unwilling to remove the bad influences from their life, this may signify a deeper issue, and that should not be ignored.

1. Jim Rohn

Chapter Three

Tactics of Manipulation

G aslighting is a term that has risen in popularity over the last few years, but what exactly is it? According to Banyan Treatment Center, gaslighting is "a form of manipulation in which one person makes the other question themselves and their sanity. People use gaslighting against others to control their thoughts, behaviors, and emotions."[1] Some warning signs of gaslighting are: lying, intimidation, mood swings, and secretive behavior. Addiction and gaslighting often go hand in hand, as it is a tactic a drug abuser may use to confuse their loved ones about what they are doing. They will manipulate circumstances and make you question your reality to distract you from their behavior.

When someone is dealing with a significant distraction, a drug addict may take advantage of the lack of attention to indulge in more substance use. Pregnancy was the perfect opportunity for my husband to take advantage of me. I was so focused on preparing for our baby and being the best possible mom, that I often neglected having conversations with Brent outside of parent talk. Nor was I paying any attention to anything he was doing. Brent loved that my mind was preoccupied because he indulged in his habits right before my eyes and it went completely unnoticed. I used the majority of my time to read baby books, clean, look up gender reveal ideas, baby shower themes, nursery room ideas, clean some more, eat, and sleep as much as possible. When Brent wasn't cooking or picking up the food I craved, his schedule consisted of working longer hours and running errands throughout the day.

He often had a surprise for me when he took longer than normal to return home. He would arrive an hour to two hours after the time he said he would and always have my favorite snacks or cook a meal for me before he left work. I rarely questioned what the holdup was because he worked at a restaurant and would communicate with me throughout his shifts. His actions reflected a working and loving husband caring for his pregnant wife. Or so I thought.

As my pregnancy progressed, I realized I had not spent much time going on dates with Brent or just enjoying his company. One afternoon, I asked if we could go out to eat. Without hesitation, he hopped up from his seat and asked what I was going to wear. We found outfits to complement each other and went to an Italian restaurant. Our lunch was filled with cheesy garlic bread, chicken fettuccine alfredo, laughter, and our son making his presence known on my bladder. We were happy and discussed planning more date nights before our little one made his grand entrance.

Time passed and we did not have the date nights we talked about. Our sleep schedules varied greatly as Brent worked at night. There were countless occasions he came home after 3:00 A.M. I expressed my dislike of his schedule and asked him to switch with someone so we could have quality time together that didn't include listening to one another snoring at different hours of the night and day. Sometimes he would make accommodations, but the majority of the time I had to just accept it for what it was.

Soon, 3:00 A.M. became 4:00 A.M. or later, and the FaceTime calls demanding he get home began. I argued that there was no way the restaurant was that busy, yet he was always able to convince me that it was. He accused that my hormones were getting the best of me, and I started to believe he was right. But my initial intuition was confirmed when one night during the week I was woken by a loud knock on our front door at 1:00 in the morning. That particular night, Brent was home and sleeping. I sat up and tapped Brent to see if he heard it too. He responded with a snore. Then a second knock occurred, and I tiptoed to the door to look through the peephole. I could not make out who it was until the person turned their head towards the door. In shock, I ran over to Brent and shook him until he woke up. "Babe, your dad is here! He's alone." Brent sprinted to the door and opened it.

"What's going on?" Brent asked. His father tried to whisper. Brent stepped outside and closed the door behind him. I made my way to the door to listen. I heard Brent suck his teeth and tell his father to wait a minute. He came back inside and started looking for his phone. I asked if everything was all right and Brent had this look on his face as if he didn't know what to say. Now just for clarification, Brent's father was not allowed to drive because of a health condition. It was concerning to us how he was able to drive to our home without his wife noticing he left. Curious, I covered up and headed to the door. When I opened it to invite my father-in-law inside, he was gone. I yelled for Brent to call his dad and even follow behind him. He called numerous times without a response then he decided to call his mother. I stood next to him and rubbed his back as he kept a hand over his head and spoke with his mother.

"Dad was just here. How did he get out of the house?" Brent said.

"I don't know!" His mom replied. "What did he want?"

Brent released a sigh and mumbled his answer.

"What did he want?" She repeated.

"He asked where he could get cocaine for Sean and Marissa's wedding this weekend."

"What?" I exclaimed as I turned him toward me. All I heard Daphne say was, "Oh God" in the most nonchalant, "here we go again" tone.

I paced the living room and rubbed my seven-month-pregnant belly. Brent asked me to sit next to him and he apologized on behalf of his father's behavior. He assured me that he was done with cocaine, as promised, and he didn't understand why his father thought he could help him. He was on the verge of tears. I comforted him and let him know he was not responsible for what his father did, but it made me very uncomfortable and if his father was involved with drugs, I didn't want him coming around our son. I suggested he talk with both of his parents the following day and afterward, the four of us could have a conversation because I had a few things I wanted to discuss with them. He was adamant that he would take care of it and he didn't want to add any further stress that could affect our son. I told him I appreciated his concern, but the situation made me very uneasy, and his father owed me an apology. I kissed him on the forehead, ending the conversation, although I didn't feel comfortable with the situation.

Days turned into weeks and before I knew it, it was our baby shower. The conversation I told him I wanted to have with his parents still had not taken place. I enjoyed my day and made minimal contact with them. This upset Brent some and I told him I still felt strongly about us needing to have a talk. He asked me to please let it go and said that he handled the situation. I didn't want to argue, so I threw my hands in the air and simply said fine. I knew he hadn't talked to them and the issue would come up again.

At my forty-week checkup, we were excited to see if I had dilated any and get an idea of when our son would be coming. My doctor informed us we needed to get to the hospital and get induced because my blood pressure was too high and with the excessive swelling I had, she was afraid I may have had preeclampsia. Without delay, we were in triage being admitted. After twenty-seven hours in labor, I had to have an emergency C-section.

Our son finally arrived, and we were overjoyed. During our time in recovery, we began noticing that our son looked a little blue. The nurses assured us he was fine and to keep using the syringe bulb to help clear his lungs. Something didn't feel right, and I kept asking the nurses if they were sure our son was okay. With certainty, they nodded their heads. I still felt something was off. Once we made it to our room and I was settled into the bed, our son began squirming around in Brent's arms. It felt like I was having an out-of-body experience when I demanded Brent hand me our son and go get help. I watched my son open his mouth with blood pouring out, tilt his head back, and turn blue. Brent screamed for the nurses and ran out of the room. I sat motionless fighting with my body to move so I could chase after them. I was still paralyzed from surgery. My mother-in-law came in and asked what happened and what she could do. All I could do was hold my stomach near my incision and cry. I couldn't get a word out. She asked if she should call my mom and I was able to nod yes.

I refused all medication the nurses offered me. I made it crystal clear I was not taking anything until after I saw my son. I sat for hours in excruciating pain until I was informed I could go to the neonatal intensive care unit (NICU). In the blink of an eye, I was, what felt like, running towards my son as he lay in a bed with multiple tubes connected to him. He was on a ventilator not breathing on his own and being pumped with fentanyl. My heart was shattered. I remember praying over him and telling him how much I loved him and how I would give anything to switch places with him. The amount of hurt was unbearable, but that was just the tip of the iceberg for what else was to come.

I spent the next few days sitting beside my son, asking questions to every healthcare provider who entered the room, on and off crying, learning to pump breast milk, and embracing the family and friends who came to visit. It was emotionally, mentally, and physically draining. On day five, the nurse practitioner asked to have a word with me in private. At the time, my best friend was the only one at the hospital with me. She stepped outside and the nurse practitioner looked at me with a serious face and said, "Mommy, the lab found traces of cocaine in his umbilical cord blood." I felt all blood flow from my face go away and immediately I heard a voice deep within my soul say "Brent." I stood looking at her and the first thing I was able to say was, "Is he okay?"

"Yes, but we have to conduct an investigation and get the Department of Children and Families involved," she said.

I told her to get them on the phone and let's begin right away. I quickly followed with a line of questioning. "Are you sure they tested my son? How can this be? Can they run the test again? Can I get a sample so I can take it to an outside lab? Who can I speak to? You guys can run whatever test you'd like on me. I have nothing to hide. There must be a mistake! I have never done cocaine." Even as I asked questions and made statements declaring my innocence, the little voice in my head kept saying I needed to start looking into Brent.

Once my best friend walked back into the room I began crying hysterically and told her what was happening. She was in disbelief and told me to call Brent. I did and instructed him to rush back to the hospital. When he arrived, he did what any concerned husband would do and consoled me. He demanded to speak with every doctor and lab technician involved in our son's case. We wanted answers, and once the two of us were alone I told him I didn't know how much more I could take. He assured me things would be fine and that there had to be a mistake. He reminded me that during labor, they did a lot of experimenting so maybe it was a result of the medication mixtures. I was too exhausted to respond, but I was at the point where I began to listen to his words closely and pay better attention to his body language. I didn't want to believe he had anything to do with what happened to our son, but I wasn't going to look past the thought, especially given his past.

By the time the Department of Children and Family (DCF) worker came to the hospital, it was just him and I in the room with my son. As he spoke, my mind wandered, thinking *this truly can't be real. I love my son more than I could ever express in words, and now I'm under investigation for something I didn't do!* Once the DCF worker stopped talking, I told him there must be a mistake and they could test me every day for the rest of my life if they wanted to. I had nothing to hide because I didn't do it. Instantaneously, he pulled out a ten-panel drug test and asked me to give him a sample. I grabbed the cup and proceeded down the hallway. It felt like a long and painful walk of shame. Nurses and other NICU parents watched me in passing and shifted their eyes to my hand. I could feel the judgment. The walk back with the cup full of urine was worse. It seemed as if the hallway filled with more bystanders and the stares were more intense.

I handed over the cup and looked at my son. His little body was surrounded by tubes and an intubator taped to his precious face. My heart was so heavy. He didn't deserve to experience this. The DCF investigator said my results were negative and he noted the information in his chart. He then began with his questions. When he asked about Brent—specifically about cocaine use—he must have noticed my attempt to protect Brent. He placed his notepad on the counter and cupped his hands together. "This process goes a lot smoother if you are honest with me," he said. I was filled with fear. I thought to myself, *what's really going to happen if I tell the truth? Will we both be under investigation and our son fall into the hands of the system? Am I going to have to fight like hell to get him back?* I've heard so many horror stories about parents' children being taken away from them, and the process to get them back takes years. I didn't want to lose any time with my child and if anything about Brent's past was documented, surely the state would get custody. Fear overpowered my better judgment and I remained loyal to my husband.

The DCF worker interviewed Brent and two other relatives of mine. He did a background check on me and walked through our home taking pictures and notes on his findings. He stated this case was very unusual. Typically, parents who are addicted to cocaine don't have diapers organized by brand and size and ask people to put on shoe covers before they step on the carpet. He said it is noticeable when there is an issue, and he didn't see the connection between me and cocaine. I was glad to hear that, but it still didn't make me feel any better as I had to deal with a drug counselor coming to speak with me about rehab services. All I wanted to focus on was my son getting better and us returning home without any of these issues. It was a continuous insult to injury. The woman who came from the rehab facility asked me specific questions about all drugs known to man. She asked what drugs I had ever used and when I used them, if I did. When she asked about cocaine, she looked up at me with her lips in a tight line. I stared into her eyes and said, "I've never done cocaine."

"It was in your son's system," she replied.

"So they said, but to answer your question, I've never done cocaine." I wasn't pleased with this woman and asked her to leave all the information she had, and I would look into it later. I felt belittled, and inside I was screaming. If only they knew me, they would never question me the way I was questioned. I was at the center of an investigation for the almost death of my son; this entire situation was too much—it was a nightmare.

My son was released exactly two weeks after he was born. I was so happy to finally get out of the hospital and begin getting accustomed to life at home. Of course, the DCF case was still open, and I was receiving random check-ins. I was informed the investigation would last roughly sixty days. It felt like an eternity! A nurse from the county even came over to watch me tend to my son. I recall how intense her stares were when I would change my son's diaper or prepare his bottle and burp him. Every move I made especially while handling my son was like a vulture staring at its next meal. I was uncomfortable in my own home.

One night Brent and I were talking, and I expressed how overwhelming this whole situation was. I was angry and lashed out as I started crying, "I'm a good person and you know just as well as anyone who knows me that I would never do something like this! I've wanted to have a baby for so long and this is how he comes into the world? Brent, I'm not trying to fight with you, but why is it that this drug keeps popping up in my life? First Carl, then my cousins, then your dad knocking on the door waking me up out of my sleep to ask you where to get some, and now it is the very thing that almost killed our son. And I'm the one who gets blamed for it? These occurrences can't be a coincidence! When's the last time you really used cocaine?"

Brent got defensive. "Are you trying to say I did this?" Internally, I said yes, but voiced the word no. I was searching for answers in his eyes. Brent took a deep breath and said, "I haven't done it since we had that big fight." He took another deep breath and continued, "Baby, I know the answer is no, but I just have to ask. Have you ever done cocaine?" His words were like a slap to my face and a punch to my gut.

"No! Never! You know that!" I replied, shocked. How could he ask me something like that?

He nodded, grabbed my hand, and said, "Okay, then we're going to get to the bottom of this together." Then he kissed me on my forehead and went to take a shower.

Red Flag #3: Gaslighting and Manipulation

Drug users use the tools of gaslighting and manipulation to take the blame and attention off of themselves and to make you question your own judgment so that you can't question their behavior. Sometimes gaslighting looks like them accusing you of the behavior that they are exhibiting, which can be very disorienting.

Manipulation is the language of guilt. Brent knew he had something to do with what happened to our son. That's why he got defensive and tried to shift the blame to me. I believe he was wrestling with knowing I was slowly connecting the dots and eventually, he was going to be the one under the spotlight. It was no coincidence that his father came asking for cocaine, knowing his son had used, and it most certainly wasn't a coincidence that two months later, that same drug somehow ended up in my system and nearly killed our son. The only way I believed it could have gotten in our son was through bodily fluid during intercourse or if it was scattered around and I was ingesting it while cleaning. Addicts will make you feel like you're crazy or going crazy! I felt like I was going crazy. That was a sign that I needed to get away from him!

I sat in our living room, frustrated and appalled he would even ask me if I'd ever done cocaine when he knew I didn't do drugs and wouldn't even drink tap water. My mind was racing, and I felt as if there were bricks continuing to pile on my shoulders. Every breath I took felt forced. I was falling into postpartum depression and didn't know it. I knew we needed to continue to talk, but I felt drained. I mustered up the strength to get up and proceeded to wash my face in the same bathroom Brent was showering in. "Are your fingers still swollen?" he asked.

I looked down. "No."

"That's good, because I have a surprise for you. I got our rings cleaned. They're in the jewelry box. Try it on and see how it fits."

I got excited and dried my hands. I opened the jewelry box and searched through it. "Where did you put them?" I asked.

"In the very front. You can't miss it," he replied.

I continued to search around and noticed several other items were missing. I began to panic. "Brent, they're not here! Neither is Donna's necklace or her ring! My sweet sixteen ring isn't here either." I opened every drawer and yelled, "The bracelets my grandfather gave me are gone! Brent, I'm missing a lot of jewelry! What the hell is going on?" Brent rushed out of the shower and joined me in looking through the jewelry box. He was just as upset as I was and kept saying he placed them in the front. His concern turned into anger, and he started questioning who could have taken it. I tried to control my breathing and placed my hand over my chest. I walked towards my son's crib and stared at him. My heart was in pain and the tears built in my eyes blurred the beautiful view of my son sleeping peacefully.

Something was wrong. I was losing trust by the day in the man I had married. I knew in my gut that he was behind the missing jewelry somehow, but I felt bad even thinking that. It was so hard to determine what was true and what was false, and I was still trying to recover from my c-section, battle postpartum depression, and not lose my mind during the DCF investigation. At that moment, I was trying to handle everything by myself; I felt the weight of the world on my shoulders, but I should've handed all my worries and cares over to God. He is who I could trust to speak truth amidst the lies and shine light in the darkness. Ephesians 4:14-15 (NIV) says, "Then we will no longer be infants, tossed back and forth by the waves, and blown here and there by every wind of teaching and by the cunning and craftiness of people in their deceitful scheming. Instead, speaking the truth in love, we will grow to become in every respect the mature body of him who is the head, that is, Christ." When we rely on the God of truth, we will not be swayed by the deceit and craftiness of people. God, through His Spirit, will reveal truth to us.

While humans deceive and manipulate, God doesn't. He is faithful through and through; His hope is an anchor for our souls. As we trust Him fully with our lived experiences, He will ground us and anchor us to truth. When in doubt, turn to Him and ask for clarity. Speak the truth of God's Word over your situation. Then when your world turns upside down and inside out, you are anchored, and you know Who you can turn to.

---

1. Alyssa. (2021, December 29). *Gaslighting and addiction - banyan treatment center palm springs*. Banyan Treatment Center. Retrieved October 6, 2022, from https://www.banyantreatmentcenter.com/2021/06/18/gaslight-and-addiction/

Chapter Four

Exposed Darkness

I t's tough to accept that someone you care about is lying or stealing from you, even when the signs are clear. You've invested a lot of time, energy, hope, and trust in this person, so it's hard to believe they could lie, steal, and hurt you so easily, right? You think the person you knew wouldn't do that, so it's difficult to understand what's happening. Addiction and drug abuse can change your loved one into a different person, altering how they act, think, and speak. It's challenging to see clearly when you've been close to and trusted this person for a long time. What might be obvious to others can be unclear to you.

After realizing that my jewelry had been stolen, I sobbed. Brent wrapped his arms around me, and I told him, "Brent, those are family heirlooms from the three people closest to me who died! I'll never get those back! I can't take this!" I continued to cry, and he continued to comfort me. He assured me we would investigate this together and we would start with maintenance because they were the only people who entered our home while we were in the hospital. I thought he had a point, and I nodded as my head pressed against his chest. Once he was able to calm me down, we proceeded to get ready for bed. I was numb. A little over two weeks prior, I was bouncing on an exercise ball to help induce labor and eating every food item that would assist in helping me dilate. I was happy. I was excited to meet my son. I thought I was in love with my life. I was ready to become a mother and make beautiful memories. This was not what I had pictured my life to be, especially after giving birth. The constant emotional and mental blows I was receiving were far too much for me to cope with. I was in pain. Physically I felt sick, and I needed help. I felt trapped and like the walls were continuing to close in on me. I told myself I would deal with the stolen jewelry in the morning and forced myself to go to sleep as my head lay on a tear-soaked pillow.

The next day, I felt like a zombie. Nothing felt okay. I couldn't even gather the strength to make a police report until my mother called me, and I told her what happened. She was just as upset as I was. You see, the three people closest to me who passed away were also the three people closest to her. Donna was her best friend and my godmother. My grandfather was her father-in-law, and the last amazing person who gave me jewelry that was stolen was my grandmother, her mother. I felt her heartbreak and her anger when she started asking questions. "When did this happen? Who has been in the apartment? Does Brent still have any friends you don't like? Do you think Brent had something to do with this?" I told her I believed it happened when I was in the hospital and the only people who came over were the maintenance workers. She urged me to call the police and file a report, which I did and sent her a text to let her know that an officer would be over within a half-hour to assist. I sent that same text to Brent. His response was supportive, and it eased my thoughts of him possibly having anything to do with this incident.

When the officer arrived, I explained to him what happened and what was missing. He looked in our bedroom and asked me to fill out a report. I listed everything I could think of that was gone and its value. The cop informed me he would speak with the leasing office and interview the maintenance crew. He also mentioned he would search the database to see if any of the items I reported missing had been taken to a pawn shop and follow up with me throughout his investigation. This took place in early October.

When November rolled around, I received a letter stating that my investigation with DCF was completed. I was happy that part of my nightmare was over, but there were still so many loose ends that I needed to tie. I opened up to certain friends who I thought could help me figure out what happened to my son. I felt shame and embarrassment as I shared what happened. Every person I confided in was in disbelief and angry. First, they were all concerned with my son's well-being and secondly, they were bothered that I went through the investigation when they knew my true character. I had friends speak to anesthesiologists and doctors about medication interactions, look over the hospital reports with me to see if there was anything that stood out, and even call lawyers regarding possible medical malpractice. We left no leaf unturned.

While I had friends assisting with the research, I proceeded to investigate my spouse. I read through countless articles about cocaine and toxicology. One article titled "Analytical Methods of Compounds in Biological Specimens: Application in Forensic Toxicology," which was published by the International Journal of Forensic Sciences, discussed drugs being excreted through sweat. Brent used to sweat a lot and I did my best to start paying attention to his behavior when he was sweating. Anytime he wasn't around, I looked through his things. I checked his drawers regularly, his shoes, and shoe boxes, I checked in the cabinets to see if anything was hidden in the back, the car he was driving, and yes, his phone while he was sleeping.

Before we started dating, I told Brent that if I ever felt the need to go through his phone, that meant I did not trust him, and that the relationship would not last. Going through someone's phone is an invasion of privacy and is a display of your lack of trust and respect for your partner. Given the magnitude of the situation, I put all of those thoughts to the side. When I heard the Lord say Brent's name in the hospital room, I was determined to get the physical evidence I needed. There was a huge problem in my household and my son experienced such a horrific entrance into this world because of it. He didn't deserve that, and I felt partially responsible because of who I chose to give him as a father. As his mother, it was my job to make things right. At the time, I believed I had to be the one to fix all the issues because that's what you do when you get married. For better or for worse, and this was beyond worse.

Red Flag #4: Lying and Stealing

A drug abuser will use whatever means necessary to keep using, including lying and stealing. At a certain point, you can't take them at their word anymore. Looking for evidence and trying to catch them in their lies becomes important to your safety and their safety.

Our wedding anniversary was approaching, and I mentioned that I was not making any plans because I felt drained. I told Brent that if we were going to do anything, it would be because he made it happen. I left the ball in his court because I wanted to see how he would respond. The day before our anniversary, he told me he arranged for my mom to babysit, and I should be ready no later than 7:00 P.M. I felt some excitement stir up inside me because he gave direction, and I was glad to comply. Brent cooked dinner for us at the restaurant he worked at and had a section closed off that was decorated with our pictures and saved wedding décor. The room was lit with dim lights and candles. My all-time favorite 90s R&B songs played from the speakers, and my favorite wine was chilled on ice next to our wedding flutes. For a moment, I was able to forget about all our problems and enjoy our celebration of love.

During dinner, Brent excused himself several times. I noticed he was a bit jittery and sweaty. I recall asking him what was on his mind, and he stated he was just excited to see my reaction to everything and was tired from all the work he put into executing his plan. After a few hours of celebration, we picked up our son and headed home. I thanked him for his efforts, told him I would let him get some rest, and that I would tend to the baby throughout the night. I dozed off soon after saying goodnight and woke up when I heard our son crying for milk.

I wiped the cold from my eyes and was shocked at the mess I saw as I made my way to the kitchen. It looked like a tornado had passed through. I quickly made our son his bottle and as I fed him, I stared into the kitchen in disbelief. I scanned the dining room table and the floor leading up to the guest bathroom. After I burped and changed our son, I grabbed my phone and started recording. Brent was knocked out with his eyes slightly open, mouth agape, and snoring. I assessed the area: a glass of wine sitting at the edge of our coffee table, the bottle on the floor, the television was left on, a vape on the bathroom counter, clothes inside the toilet, a towel thrown on the floor between the living room and front entrance, a trash bag sitting on one of the kitchen counters, a gallon of orange juice next to it, waffles on a plate sitting on the stove, spilled formula on the counter, trash overflowing, a loaf of bread left open on another counter top, cut up red potatoes, an open bottle with formula still inside, dirty dishes on the counter and in the sink, and bread laying out on the other side of the sink. I took a deep breath and started cleaning. I wanted so badly to wake him up and say something, but I knew it wouldn't do any good at that time. In the bathroom, I examined the vape and smelled marijuana. I looked for traces of white residue and searched through his drawers to see if he had anything that lined up with what happened to our son. I didn't find anything, so I washed my hands and headed back to sleep.

When Brent woke up the next afternoon, I eased what happened into conversation. I remained calm and showed him the video and asked what he was thinking. We had a huge meal for dinner, so I didn't understand why he created such a mess. He played his part and made shocked expressions as he watched the video. He turned to me to say he had no idea he did any of that.

There's that red flag again. He didn't drink much wine at dinner, and he didn't have any other alcoholic beverages. I have been around him before when he smoked marijuana and he never made a mess like that. This was different. I knew he was hiding something. I just wasn't sure how I wanted to proceed, and not have it turn into an argument. I just wanted physical proof.

Brent apologized and thanked me for cleaning up and not being upset. He was wrong. I was very upset, but I didn't show it. I didn't want to fight.

The days and nights seemed to blend—every day the same but with the addition of more stress. I checked the funds in my bank account and when I mentioned to Brent that my maternity pay was up, he became worried. I remember asking him why he was acting like it was an issue when we had this discussion as soon as we found out I was pregnant. He said he was simply surprised by how quickly my maternity pay finished and not to worry, because he was going to take care of everything as planned.

When December rolled around, I asked him to deposit his money into my bank account so I could give the leasing office a check. He couldn't make eye contact with me. He said he didn't have any money. Anger rushed through my body.

Brent explained how he spent so much money on gas from traveling back and forth to the hospital, his job, all of our son's follow-up appointments, and on formula. I lost my cool and argued with him that there was no way that was possible because I had been helping pay for those things and he had nine months to save, so we wouldn't be in the very situation we were in. I was past being pissed off. He kept trying to calm me down and said he would ask his mother for the money. That turned into another fight. The last thing I wanted was for either of our parents to get involved in our finances. I told him he needed to figure it out quickly because rent was due the next day.

The next morning Brent said he could ask one of his grandmothers for help. I recall looking up at the ceiling thinking, *what drug is he on? Lord, please help me out because this is too much.* I firmly said no and asked him what his other options were. He told me he asked his mother, and she wasn't able to help, and his boss couldn't write him an advance. He said he was out of ideas, grabbed his phone, and went on social media.

I sat there thinking, *How in the world is nine months not enough time to save for one to two months' worth of rent? He is obviously spending money recklessly. I know it is drugs. I just need proof.*

I was at a fork in the road. With everything that had transpired, I needed to breathe. I needed to vent. I needed to scream. I needed help and fast. I prayed and fought back tears, wondering why this was happening and why couldn't my husband be more responsible. Especially during this time. I needed him to be the strong one. I needed him to figure it out while I healed. The stress was overwhelming.

I called my best friend, Natalie. When she answered, I told her everything. I could feel her anger towards my husband. "What the hell is he spending his money on and why do you have to be the one to figure out how to fix the situation he caused? Is he serious? You did all the preparations while you were pregnant! You had an emergency c-section! You were under investigation for something you didn't do! Not one bit of your maternity leave has been normal and now you have this added on. He needs to step up and get it together! You're not going to stress anymore. Tell me how much you need, and I've got you. Don't worry about paying me back asap. I know you will, but you don't need this stress! How dare he do this to you guys!" I was sobbing by the time she finished yelling. She was absolutely right. She continued to say her peace until I gave her a total. She transferred the funds immediately and told me she sent extra for groceries, gas, and formula. "If you need more, you call me! Don't you dare go to a cash advance place. I love you."

When Brent got home, I told him he needed to call Natalie and say thank you. Instead, he grabbed the remote. I took it away and turned off the television. "We need to have a discussion about finances and your future checks. It is embarrassing that I had to figure this out and call my best friend to ask for what you should have handled. You don't seem to understand just what you've done. Where has all your money been going?" Brent didn't have a specific answer. He kept saying he spent it, and he was sorry. I continued, "You spent it and you're sorry? That's not good enough. When your next check comes in, you're going to hand it over to me so I can budget and begin paying Natalie back. You're going to open a bank account and stop living in the stone age and show that you can be responsible. I can't believe that we are even having to have this conversation. Do you even want to be married?"

Brent sat up and looked me dead in the eye. "Yes, I'm going to give you all my checks from here on, and yes, I want to be married. I messed up and I'm going to do whatever is necessary to fix this. Jess, I'm so sorry." He cried and so did I.

We continued to talk about our marriage, where it was going, and how we were going to fix it. We made a plan to move forward and vowed to stick to it. It was rough initially. Very rough. It was hard not to continue to bring up past issues when trying to move forward. The past continued to replay in the back of my mind to prepare me for the next time it happened—*if* it happened—so it wouldn't hurt as bad. We tried doing nice things for one another during this time and when he received his check, he handed it over so I could deposit it into my bank account. We communicated with each other how the money would be spent and stuck to the plan. A weight was lifted off my shoulders, and I thought things were on the up and up. We were talking with one another more, enjoying our son as he hit milestones, and working on our intimacy. It seemed like there was finally a break from all the chaos.

Things were changing for the better until one day I went downstairs to get something I had forgotten from my car. After I retrieved the item, there was a gut-wrenching feeling that overpowered me and led me to Brent's vehicle. I punched in the code and opened the driver-side door. I was disgusted. There were empty black and mild wrappers, marijuana stems, empty cigarette cartons, lighters, empty black bags that you get from the liquor store, dirt and ashes everywhere, clothes piled in the front and back seat, and in the center console, I saw gold. My heart started racing as I reached in to grab the gold. There it was—two of the six bracelets I reported missing.

I shut my eyes for a moment, taking deep breaths to calm my anger. I was shaking and needed to get myself together. Looking at the state of the car made me realize that Brent had a bigger problem than I had thought. I couldn't go back upstairs still upset, so I took out my phone and started recording. After that, I opened the trunk to see what was inside. I found more garbage, cans of formula, clothes in bags that I had asked him to donate months ago, and a pair of women's sweatpants neatly folded that I had never seen before. I unfolded them and examined them closely; they definitely weren't mine. Once again, I felt like everything was falling apart. Brent had been hiding so much from me. This person was not who I thought I married.

When a loved one is abusing drugs, they bring so much darkness into their life and yours. They begin to behave in ways you don't recognize such as lying, cheating, and stealing. This darkness casts a shadow over your relationship and it can be hard to imagine what the future will bring, if things will get better, and how to move forward.

Ephesians 5:8-13 (NIV) tells us, "For you were once darkness, but now you are light in the Lord. Live as children of light (for the fruit of the light consists in all goodness, righteousness, and truth) and find out what pleases the Lord. Have nothing to do with the fruitless deeds of darkness, but rather expose them. It is shameful even to mention what the disobedient do in secret. But everything exposed by the light becomes visible—and everything that is illuminated becomes a light." Everything will be exposed to the light. When you catch your loved one in a lie or have an intuition that they might be lying, know that one day, everything will be exposed by the light.

It is also important to remember that what man uses for evil, God can use for good (Genesis 50:20); what man does in darkness, God can redeem by His light. God rebuilds, redeems, and restores. So when you feel hopeless about the life you envisioned and the future you desired, seek solace in Him and confide in Him completely. Though you may not be able to see it right now, your future is full of light.

Chapter Five
The Blame Game

Brent was connected to all the chaos and distress I experienced, but he kept denying it. I was in shock. How could I believe him when I had already found all of the evidence? He was lying to my face. Yes, I wanted him to be clean and I wanted to be able to trust him to care for me and our family. But *wanting* something to be true is not the same as truth. A drug abuser will capitalize on your desires and beliefs at the expense of your well-being. If your loved one prioritizes their drug of choice over you and your well-being, even going to lengths to blame you and create distance in your relationship to continue their behavior, then they are more committed to their drug than you. That's something you have to come to terms with.

I took a moment to soak in the reality of the situation. I was battling my inner thoughts. *I know there's a drug issue that is being uncovered, but now infidelity? He would never cheat on me. I know we have had our fair share of arguments and then some, but cheating? After all we've been through? Is this part of the reason why he doesn't have money? It adds up, but my husband loves me, and he knows that would break me. There has to be some logical explanation for this, but my intuition is saying there's someone else. Keep calm, grab the items, and confront him. You're not a dummy and he's playing you like a fool. This has to end. The old Jessica wouldn't put up with this! Bring her out!*

After searching Brent's car, I walked towards the stairs to get to the apartment door. Each step felt heavier than the next. My heart was pounding so hard I felt it in my throat. My face was hot and my eyes welled with tears. I closed my eyes and wiped them before they could roll down. My breath caught as I placed my hand on the doorknob and turned it to enter. There he was, standing in the kitchen in front of the stove, cooking our lunch. Our son was asleep in his bassinet by the couch. Brent asked me if I was ready to eat. I stood staring at him, trying to control my breathing and avoid having an outburst. I held up the bracelets between my fingers. I didn't take my eyes off him. "These were in the center console of the green car. Any idea why they would be there?"

Brent quickly responded, "You must have put them there and forgot about it."

"No," I sharply answered.

Brent continued, "Then maybe I was using it for good luck when I went to play poker with the guys and just forgot about it."

I nodded. "Yeah, maybe. But what about the women's sweatpants that are in the trunk of the car?"

Brent kept a straight face and said, "You do know the clothes that you wanted me to drop off are still there, right? Maybe they fell out."

I smiled and shook my head. "That's not possible, because they were neatly folded on top of one of the bags, and I know my clothes. They're not mine, so whose are they?" Immediately, the mood changed, and I was under the spotlight.

"What are you trying to say, Jessica? I didn't steal your jewelry. I know how much that means to you." I just stood in place staring at him, making him uncomfortable with my silence. He continued, "You always have something to say and now you choose to be quiet? Speak." I smiled and continued to stare. "You really think I took your jewelry? Well, I didn't!"

I smiled and said, "Sure you didn't."

That set him off! "You're really going to blame me for stealing your jewelry? Those bracelets aren't even worth much. You know, you have a problem with everything and everyone. I don't do anything right in your eyes, you don't like my friends, you don't like my family, and you are always nagging about cleaning. You make me not want to be here. You don't know how to just stop. Nothing is ever good enough for you."

That was the end of my silence. "What does any of that have to do with my jewelry ending up in the car you drive and a pair of women's sweatpants being in the trunk? Whose are they?"

"They're yours! Whose else would they be?" he yelled.

"Right, they're mine. And how exactly would you know what the bracelets are worth if you didn't take them somewhere for an estimate?" I asked with my eyebrow raised.

"I'm trying to work on our marriage and cook us lunch so we can spend time together and you're looking for an argument. Why do you always want to argue?" He shook his head, grabbed plates, and began serving our food as if what we were discussing wasn't a big deal.

Red Flag #5: Passing the Blame

Drug abusers keep control of the situation by shifting blame onto you or accusing you of playing a role in what's happening. When they push the weight of responsibility onto you, they are trying to distract you and pull your energy away from catching them in their lies and choices. They know they've been caught and they're not ready to deal with the consequences, so they are going to do everything in their power to make you rethink what you know is true.

We ate without exchanging any words. Afterward, the cleanup was quiet. We sat in front of the TV in silence. The only time the silence broke was when our son cried, and we had to attend to his needs. We played with him, took pictures, and just stared at him. But between us, there was little eye contact and very few words, mostly related to our son. It felt like darkness was returning to our home, and I could sense myself sinking into a depressed state. The pain lingered, and I felt numb once again. I wished I could wake up from this recurring nightmare, but no matter what I thought was the right thing to do, I felt trapped. I began questioning why I deserved this life. Praying became difficult; I couldn't find the words to talk to God. I felt ashamed and embarrassed. My thoughts were filled with questions: *How does a college-educated woman find herself in this position? Was I so desperate for love that I settled, when I actually deserved better than what I was receiving? Why was I having such a hard time standing up and walking away? Why was I allowing myself to continue to deal with this mess? What part did I play? Did I make him this way? Surely, I must have set off a trigger in him.* The more I continued to think, the deeper I fell into hopelessness.

As Christmas approached, I tried to keep my spirits up for the sake of making our son's first Christmas a memorable one. Brent was working late hours and I was going back to work. My heart was heavy. With all that had happened, the last place I wanted to be was at work, where everyone would have questions about how life was going as a new mom. My experience wasn't normal, and I found it hard to focus on the positives. My life was in turmoil and the only reason I kept pushing was for my son's sake.

I made the most of the holiday season and when the new year came, Brent and I tried to rekindle our relationship. Again, I accused him of using drugs, stealing, and infidelity and he continued to deny everything. Our conversations weren't going anywhere. We were stuck going in circles. Crying. Yelling. Silence. More crying. More yelling. More silence. We acted as if nothing had happened the day before, then right back to the cycle. Day in and day out. I was drained physically, mentally, and emotionally. Spiritually, I was the thirstiest I had ever been but felt so out of reach from the fountain. There were moments of closeness that seemed to fill the time or bring some pleasure to feel alive. Occasionally, it provided some comfort, but more often, I felt a sense of disconnection. Most of the time, Brent was under the influence of marijuana. It didn't feel like we were expressing love; it felt more like fulfilling an obligation.

One night we found ourselves in a heated argument. We said some of the most hurtful things we've ever said to each other. I harped on all the problems of our past, his drug abuse, his lousy choice of friends, and his ir-responsible nature. I mentioned him learning these habits from his father. I told him the proof was in that visit his father made to our apartment in the middle of the night. "The apple didn't fall too far from the tree, and I'll be damned if our apple turns out anything like you!"

Brent was furious and with all seriousness in his voice and face, he said to me, "You can't talk. You didn't even give birth the right way." I stood there with my mouth open, speechless. I took steps back until I felt the couch behind me and sat down. Crying, I called him every name under the sun. He continued, "This is why my friends and family don't like you! You think you're better than everyone else! You think you know everything! Your crap stinks too! Why do you think I rather be at work? Because coming home to you and your nagging is the last place I want to be! You're always accusing me of something. You're always looking for something that's not there. You like drama and don't know how to chill out! You're the problem!"

I wept. Part of me believed his words. I felt myself shrinking into the couch. His words became muffled as I zoned out, wondering how we had fallen so far from where we once stood. This isn't who I thought I knew. Surely the devil was attacking our union. This was all too much. I needed to get out, but I didn't know how to ask for help.

I had so many thoughts rushing through my head. Although Brent was convincing, I knew he was lying, and he was trying to shift the blame off of himself. This is typical behavior for drug abusers. It's a transfer of guilt. This is when you need to cling to your intuition. This is when God is speaking to you and giving you the opportunity to make wise decisions on how to proceed.

When you are in a relationship with a drug abuser who is unwilling to change and come clean, it can feel like you're on a battlefield. This is when we tend to overthink and make wrong choices because we want to continue giving the benefit of the doubt to our fleshly desire to stay committed to a situation that is no longer serving us. I knew something was very wrong, but I couldn't face the thought of actually leaving. Though the spirit inside me wasn't at peace, I tried to press on.

When your loved one is unwilling to change their behavior and starts blaming you for the consequences of their actions, they are bringing you into their destruction. Proverbs 11:3 (ESV) says, "The integrity of the upright guides them, but the crookedness of the treacherous destroys them." Honestly, Brent was destroying his life and pulling me into the destruction. This is where so many of us fold because we perceive letting go as being harder than holding on to what we already know. The fear of the unknown creeps in and makes itself comfortable as we contemplate what's happening to us. In my case, I became committed to discovering all the whys and hows rather than following my intuition and removing myself from the situation. I wanted to help my ex-husband fight his demons. This wasn't who I married, and I wanted the man I thought I knew to come back. It was a battle that was not meant for me to take on.

When the drug abuser is passing blame, it can be frustrating to have their behavior projected onto you. When this happens, cling to the truth that your integrity will guide you. God sees and knows everything. He sees through people's actions and into their hearts. When you feel unfairly blamed, do not take that on as part of your identity. Instead, hand that burden to God and let His justice and promises fill you with hope.

Chapter Six

The Tightrope of Unpredictability

E ach of us can be impulsive on occasion. We go for the fries instead of the veggies, we decide to stay up one hour past our bedtime, or we get a drastic haircut. But when impulsive behavior becomes habitual, that's when it becomes an issue. This is where addiction's vice-like grip comes in. What was once an impulsive decision to do drugs or have another drink becomes a consistent habit that begins to have control over other areas of the user's life. Not only does this affect future decisions, but it also affects the brain. According to an article titled "The Connection Between Impulsive Behavior and Addiction," Genesis Recovery writes, "Drug and alcohol use weakens the prefrontal cortex, making you more likely to act impulsively. Continued impulsive behavior, especially when left untreated, can develop into an addiction."[1] The prefrontal cortex is the part of the brain that helps you make rational decisions and when that is compromised, it puts your loved one and you in a dangerous position.

There were ebbs and flows with Brent's behavior. There were times when I felt like things were finally calming down and getting back to "normal," but then shortly after, they would take a turn for the worse.

Some semblance of peace was made when Brent handed over his next paycheck. I deposited it into my account and took care of the bills. We hardly spoke, but eventually, we started to act as husband and wife again. He hugged me and whispered, "Sorry," in my ear. I apologized too. We took turns cooking for one another and our discussions often led to him needing a new car. He mentioned his supervisor had a dealership and was willing to work with him so he could get a car sooner than later. He explained the details and I froze when he asked for $200 to make a deposit on the car. He continued to explain why he needed it and showed me the text messages between him and his supervisor. I thought about it long and hard. Brent continued to persuade me. I didn't want to say yes, but since he was giving me his paychecks, we had the funds, and I figured this would be his opportunity to show me he was trying to do better.

I took a deep breath and handed him the money. I told him he needed to show me a receipt for the deposit. He said he would, thanked me, kissed me, and told me not to cook because he was going to bring dinner for us. He left around 5:00 P.M. and sent me pictures of potential cars, once he was at the dealership.

As it grew later into the evening, I started texting him to ask when he would be home because I was getting hungry. He said he was finishing up, then he would head to the restaurant to cook our meals. When I asked him to hurry, he said he would, and that he wouldn't be much longer. I watched television until I fell asleep and woke when my son needed a bottle. I looked at the time and it was after 11:00 P.M. I called Brent. No answer. I texted him. Minutes later, no answer. I called him again. Still no answer. He finally called me back a few moments later apologizing and said he was on his way. I hung up and rocked my son in the recliner, tracing the outline of his face. I told him how much I loved him. Despite being upset with Brent, I chose to focus on how precious my son was. Everything made sense looking into his beautiful brown eyes. I didn't feel hungry, and I didn't care what excuses Brent was going to feed me once he walked in the door. I was at peace bonding with my son and yet felt so much guilt for not feeling like this more often.

Brent finally arrived a few minutes after midnight. He was empty-handed, and his eyes were bloodshot red. The combination of alcohol and marijuana oozed from his pores, and his breath when he spoke. He was jittery. I knew he was drunk and high, but this was more than a marijuana high. He'd never been this amped up around me before. He couldn't stay in one spot while he was talking. He began with excuses of why he was held up and why he didn't arrive with any food. I was livid, but my son was in my arms, and I wasn't going to do anything to startle him. I shook my head and told Brent not to worry, to please take a shower, and get some rest. He kept pacing from the front door of our son's room to the opposite side of the apartment. He kept talking. I tried to be nice to him and asked him to shower once more. I told him I would have a bottle of water waiting for him so he could drink when he got out. He nodded and kept talking gibberish. Things changed when he stepped back inside the room, looked at me, and said, "Just so you know, if you ever take my son away from me, I'll make you disappear."

He didn't move from the opening of our son's bedroom door. His eyes normally blue, loving, and inviting, were now dark, demonic, and empty. I tightened my grip around our son and told him, "You need to leave. Now. Get out!" I locked eyes with his and had a stare down. My heart was racing. Fear and courage battled inside me. Every movement he made, I followed closely. I wasn't sure what he was going to do or say next, but I was determined to make sure no harm came our son's way.

He paced around mocking me while he grabbed some clothes. He could barely walk straight as he headed for the front door. He took all the phone chargers, and I jumped seeing him heading for the car keys next. My son was in my arms. I set him in his crib and took the car keys. I yelled at Brent, telling him that if he dared take either car, I would call the cops. He mocked me one final time, stumbled out the door, and left it open. As I proceeded to close the door and lock it, I felt the room begin to spin. With my back against the door, I cried out to God, "Lord, what just happened?"

Red Flag #6: Impulsive Behavior

A drug abuser will begin acting impulsively and reacting rather than thoughtfully responding to conflict. When unpredictable and impulsive behavior and words become the norm, your loved one is putting you in a dangerous and precarious situation.

I checked on our son to make sure he was still asleep, then grabbed my phone to make a call. I knew I needed help, but I didn't know who to call. It was late, and I didn't want to wake anyone up or involve anyone else in our marital problems. I fought with my inner thoughts. A part of me was saying to keep this between the two of us and another part was screaming to ask for help. I started to realize this was more than inviting someone into our marital problems. This was about him bringing drugs into our home and endangering me and our son. Particularly our son. Enough was enough. It was time for me to make a choice and stop trying to solve problems bigger than I could handle. I decided to call Natalie. I quickly explained to her what happened and asked if she was able to come over because Brent had taken all the phone chargers and my battery was significantly low. Without hesitation, she got dressed and headed over.

For the first time, I spilled *everything* about all our problems. Natalie sat with her jaw dropped and repeatedly said, "No way." She understood why I didn't want to involve anyone, but assured me that this situation needed intervention. This wasn't a battle I could fight through alone. I needed help. We spoke for hours, and she convinced me I needed to ask my parents for help. I expressed to her that I was afraid they were going to hate him. I was afraid that if we were able to work past this situation, they would forever hold it over his head. She looked me square in my eye, tapped on the table, and said, "You're going to hate yourself more if you don't speak up and something else happens to your son. You're focusing on the wrong thing."

She was right. When you're not thinking clearly, you begin to focus on all the inconsequential things. His behavior was completely and unequivocally irrational. It was extremely impulsive, and it was nonetheless dangerous. This was a major red flag and this time I acted on my impulse. I was able to trust my instinct at the right time. However, there are so many others who don't. How you respond to the red flag can be fear-based or a result of how you're accustomed to the behavior. Whether it's you or someone you know in this position, I urge you to realize this is NOT okay and it's time to remove yourself from the situation!

I was exhausted by the time the sun came out. I didn't sleep and Natalie had to leave to get ready for work. She reminded me to stay strong and to speak with my parents. She assured me it was best for me and my son. Moments after she left, I packed my son's diaper bag and made the call I was dreading. When my mom answered, I simply asked if they were home and if we could come over. Like a typical grandmother, she was excited and told us to come by. When we pulled into the driveway, my mom was already running to the car. I knew the smile on her face was going to be short-lived and I hated that.

As soon as we got situated inside, she asked me what was wrong. I took a deep breath and shared what happened the night before. "I have to leave him," I told her. "He's becoming too unpredictable and I'm not going to have my son thinking this behavior is normal. I've tolerated enough."

My mother went straight into mommy mode, grabbed her purse, and began putting my son in his car seat. "We are going to the hardware store to change the locks. Over my dead body will he be coming around my daughter and my grandson like that! What happened to Aries was because of him! It all makes sense now! You did the right thing, and you should be proud of yourself."

The locks were changed not long after. I had dinner with my family and announced I was going to leave Brent. I had their full support and felt relieved. The next day, Brent called me to ask why his key wouldn't open the door. I told him I changed the locks, and we were separated. There were a lot of nasty words exchanged and I ended the conversation letting him know I would have all his clothes ready for pick up later that night. When I told him he could get his things, he texted me stating his mother, brother, and sister-in-law would be picking up his belongings. They arrived, and I apologized to them for having to come over under the circumstances and explained what was going on. I showed his mother the video of the car and told her he was responsible for my jewelry missing.

She shook her head in disbelief. "Pawning jewelry is one of his old, old, old habits. I thought he was past that."

I stood and said, "Apparently, it's still something he does. When he's done spending our money, he has to find another way to support his drug habit and I have to do what I feel is best to protect myself and my son."

They gathered all his belongings and left.

In the following weeks, I arranged for Brent to meet me at the park so he could spend time with our son. I didn't want him in the apartment, and I didn't feel comfortable being alone with him. During our scheduled visits and in our phone conversations and texts, I kept things brief and wasn't very friendly. I tried to appear strong and unaffected until one day a text from him caught me off guard. He simply asked if I had gotten my period. I replied, "No, it's because of all the stress. I'm not pregnant." I sat back and thought about the possibility all day until I finally went to the pharmacy and purchased a test.

When morning came, I went straight to the bathroom. I kept telling myself I was good and not to worry. Once the test was on the counter, I cleaned up and started washing my hands. I stared in the mirror, trying to see if I noticed any physical differences, as I did before, but I was four months postpartum, so it was hard to tell. I looked down and saw the test was still loading. In my previous experiences, when the test took that long to load, it usually came back negative. I was feeling great until I took a second look and saw the word "pregnant." I screamed, "Oh my God!" Immediately, I started crying. My son was in the next room giggling in his crib. So many emotions emerged as I searched for my phone. I was scared, angry at myself, and slightly joyful. I always wanted my children to be close in age, but never did I think I would have them back-to-back! Never did I think I would be in the situation I was in. I was newly separated, and dealing with a drug-addicted husband. Having another baby was not on my to-do list. I was already upset about having to figure out how to schedule visitations and looking into divorce attorneys, let alone have another baby come into the mix. Once again, my thoughts went wild, and thinking about having two children living in a broken home tugged on my heart. This wasn't supposed to be this way. I knew I needed to tell Brent, but the first person I called was my sister. I called my mom next, and she three-wayed my father into our call. Surprisingly, no one was upset. They told me it was going to get rough, but my kids would have each other and this baby was going to provide me with something I was missing. My mom made sure I understood this new baby was a blessing and was supposed to come, and that I needed to accept it and be grateful. I felt better, but I still needed to tell Brent.

I sent Brent a text telling him I was on my way to his job, and that he needed to come outside. When I arrived, he came over to my car and I handed him the pregnancy test. He let out a heavy sigh, rubbed his forehead, and said, "I knew it." I told him I was keeping this baby and I would have a doctor's appointment coming up the following week. He asked when I believed I was due. "Most likely October," I told him.

He looked at me and said, "So our kids are going to be 13 months apart."

I cried again. Then I yelled at him and myself. The tears kept flowing. Brent grabbed my hand and spoke softly, assuring me everything was going to be okay. I was vulnerable. I felt comfort in the tone of his voice as I had so many times before and slowly, my guard began to come down. "This whole situation is messed up! How is it going to be all right? We're not even living together anymore. I can't trust you. Look at our lives!" Brent did what Brent does best. He was able to convince me that he was wrong for everything that had taken place and that he was going to set things right. Once again, I wanted so badly to believe him and to regain some sort of normalcy in my life. I wanted my family. I wanted all the ugly and old to leave and a new beginning to emerge. I was looking for hope in a situation so hopeless. I caved in and agreed we would try again.

As time went on, I found myself being extremely cautious. I didn't give Brent a spare key, but I allowed him to stay overnight. I wasn't comfortable letting him be alone with our son. I firmly told him that he needed to prove himself. This seemed to work in my favor until Brent started making comments about me being too controlling and how I needed to trust him.

I wasn't ready to trust him completely because he still needed to earn it. Some days he was sweet and other days he threw tantrums. His tantrums ranged from huffing and puffing when I asked him to make a bottle or change a diaper in the middle of the night to storming out of the apartment mid-sentence because he didn't like a facial expression I gave him when he was saying something questionable. His behavior was all over the place, and I was starting to feel exhausted again. He always made sure I knew I was bothering him and claimed I asked too many questions. We had another big argument when he saw me searching through the trash. He called his mom to pick him up, and within fifteen minutes, he was gone. I tried my best to stay calm and not let his actions bother me until he started calling me, asking why I didn't chase him before he left. It was ridiculous. I finally got angry enough to tell him to stay at his mom's until he could prove to be the man our family needed.

When his birthday rolled around, he said he was going to come by to celebrate with me and our son. I cooked his favorite meal and dressed us up. We waited, and waited, and waited, until he texted me he wasn't going to be able to come. I was livid. I didn't talk to him for a few days and when I did, I went off on him. He didn't care about anything I had to say. He was very dismissive, and I started feeling like he was using again.

Not too long after, I felt a strong pull inside, telling me I needed to call Brent's probation officer. I did and left a voicemail. I felt another tug tell me to call the detective who investigated the stolen jewelry. I couldn't find peace until I followed my intuition. When the detective answered my call, I simply asked him to run Brent's name in the database to see if he was responsible for it. He was confused and asked why. I explained I had major suspicions of his drug use, and had found 2 bracelets in the car, but I wanted confirmation on all the other items. He assured me he would investigate it. Five minutes later he called. "Mrs. Lewis, this is

Detective Green calling you back. Yeah, I just ran your husband's name and it's all here. It was him." He told me the location of the pawn shop. It was a pawn shop that was conveniently located across the street from a neighborhood well known for its drug activity. He read off the items Brent had pawned and the dates. I was speechless. He had been pawning items I wasn't even aware of since we began dating. Hurt, anger, and frustration were becoming normal feelings for me, and impulsive, unpredictable, and lying behaviors continued for him.

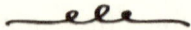

When you are in a relationship with someone who is exhibiting impulsive behavior, it can be very scary. Proverbs 14:17 (TPT) says, "An impulsive person has a short fuse and can ruin everything, but the wise show self-control." You can't predict what your loved one is going to do, which steals peace of mind from you and can ruin your relationship. You constantly feel paranoid and uncertain. In these moments, it's important to remember that the God of peace is with you and He will guard you. Philippians 4:6-7 (ESV) says, "Do not be anxious about anything, but in everything by prayer and supplication with thanksgiving let your requests be made known to God. And the peace of God, which surpasses all understanding, will guard your hearts and your minds in Christ Jesus." Make your requests known to Him. Share your feelings about the behavior of your loved one and how it's affecting you. Ask for His provision and guidance. It's impossible to predict an addict's actions but you can protect your heart and mind by seeking God's peace and presence. Additionally, you can start developing a strategy to create a safe space and distance yourself.

1. "The Connection between Impulsive Behavior and Addiction." Genesis Recovery. Accessed October 24, 2022. https://www.genesisrecovery.com/impulsive-behavior-and-drug-addiction/

Chapter Seven

Abuse Unmasked

Recognizing the various forms of abuse becomes challenging when you're deeply entangled in it, particularly when the abuser constantly blames you and instills doubt about your own experiences. For me, one of the toughest aspects of this journey was openly acknowledging the abuse. Claiming this pain can be incredibly hard for several reasons. It might make us feel vulnerable, as if we're playing the victim. There's a tendency to believe that what we've been through isn't as bad as someone else's experience, leading to a sense of not deserving to call it abuse. Phrases like "at least he didn't hit me..." or "at least she didn't completely abandon me..." undermine and dismiss the gravity of the abuse suffered, hindering the healing process. Taking the step to claim it is the initial stride towards freedom, and to be honest, it took me a while to get there.

As I progressed in my pregnancy, the distance between Brent and me grew. I managed to smile and share my excitement for my new son with others, but deep down I was in sorrow. Every night, I cried myself to sleep when Brent wasn't with me. I felt guilty for my sons being surrounded by my grief. I felt I wasn't a good mother for allowing Brent to pull my strings as if he were a puppet master. My children didn't deserve for me to allow him to have such a hold on me, but he did. I mourned the life

I thought I was going to have. Every other day, we were arguing about something. It didn't matter what it was. Confrontation was a part of our communication. I often reminded him of all the wrongs he had done and accused him of cheating on me. By this time, Brent had admitted he experimented with ecstasy and my suspicions of there being another woman rose again. He was so far gone from the person I thought I knew.

There was one night he stayed over to spend time with our son and help me throughout the night. That night, I was in pain and having difficulty getting off the bed to make our son his bottle. I tapped his shoulder several times and called his name. Each time, he would groan and wave for me to stop. Our son was crying, and I continued trying to wake him. My back was spasming, and I had uterine cramps. I was just about in tears and resumed nudging him. "Brent, please. I really need your help! Go make Aries his bottle." Brent was fed up and yelled at me to do it myself. I screamed at him, "You're so selfish!" as I managed to force myself into the kitchen. While feeding our son, I watched Brent sleep. I was disgusted with him. Who was this person he had become? He used to want children so bad and there we were with a baby boy and another growing in my stomach. This is what we wanted and there I was, doing it all and not receiving help from him.

I continued to allow him to overstep boundaries until the boundaries were no longer visible. Every time I said I had enough, I gave him another chance. He knew how to play with my emotions and then mastered manipulating my mind. And so the cycle continued. My self-confidence was low. I didn't feel I deserved better because of what happened to my eldest son. I chose to give someone a chance and I felt this was my payback for making the wrong decision. At that time, I didn't believe there was any abuse taking place because he hadn't put his hands on me. However, physical abuse was taking place because he knew I was pregnant again, had a previous cesarean, and my body was in overdrive. Back-to-back pregnancies take a toll on your body and there are physical limitations. Because he was not helping me like he should have, I was compromising my unborn, myself, and my son. This was physical abuse.

Red Flag #7: Abuse

Abuse comes in many forms and when you're not mentally strong enough, you will continue to allow it. We teach others how to treat us by what we accept. Whether the abuse is verbal, emotional, physical, or spiritual, every form of abuse is damaging and should not be overlooked or dismissed.

I laid our son in between us and tried to comfort myself, as I was still in pain. Brent adjusted himself and rolled over. I reached over to push him back so he wouldn't roll on top of our son and Brent opened his eyes and yelled, "You fat witch!" This started an argument that ended when our son woke up crying.

Brent was becoming bolder with his verbal abuse. He did not care about what he said or how he said things to me. He continued telling me how much of a witch I was and then turned around and apologized for hurting my feelings. I became numb to it and eventually tuned him out. One day we were good and the next we weren't. My suspicions of his drug use grew more with each passing day, but I decided not to think about it for fear of having a miscarriage. My gut constantly spoke to me, and I constantly ignored it. I didn't want to entertain the thought of another traumatic incident happening with my second son. I tried to focus on just me and my children. It was difficult. I knew he was using, and I couldn't prove it.

Brent settled into a routine of coming around for a few consecutive days, then disappearing only to repeat the cycle.

Once I was nine months pregnant, I started losing my patience with Brent. We had arrangements for him to come over for breakfast one day, and thirty minutes before he was to arrive, he sent me a text saying someone he was in close contact with was sick and he wasn't going to come around until after he was tested. I vividly remember a sense of urgency rushing through my body. I knew he was lying, and I knew this was the time to catch him. I tried texting and calling him back multiple times. He did not respond until six hours later.

When he returned my call, I was in the middle of talking to his probation officer, providing a statement in person. I indicated that Brent would likely test positive for marijuana, but I wasn't certain about the presence of other drugs. I voiced my suspicions, pointing towards cocaine and pills. His probation officer asked me if I was prepared for this getting back to Brent and I said, "Yes, but please not until after I give birth. I need him tested immediately, but don't show him the statement until after I deliver my son."

As I drove off, I called Brent back. He apologized for not responding in a timely manner and for scaring me. I tried to play it off as if it wasn't a big deal. He asked me to wait a minute because he had a call coming in from his probation officer. My heart began to pound. When he came back on the line, he told me he wouldn't be able to come with me to my ultrasound the next day because he had to meet with him. I acted surprised and said I would be sure to send pictures. That night, I didn't get much sleep because I knew all hell was going to break loose the next day.

Brent sent me loving text messages throughout my ultrasound appointment. That changed when he met with his probation officer. He began sending me nasty messages, accusing me of being the one who got him drug tested. He was furious. I tried to act like it wasn't me and he began accusing my mother. Once I left my ultrasound appointment, I called his probation officer to get information about their interaction. They informed me Brent was pissed and admitted to using marijuana. They said his results came back positive for marijuana and they were going to send samples to a lab for further testing.

The last month of my pregnancy was met with a complete disconnect from Brent. He never wanted to come around and he rarely called or texted me, let alone checked in on our son. I was a legally married single mother and had been the entire pregnancy. The reality of it all sunk in the night before I was admitted to the hospital. I prayed nothing would go wrong this time around. Fear and sadness overtook me when I should have been excited to meet my new son.

At the hospital, I was induced and once I reached five centimeters of dilation, I called and texted Brent to let him know. He showed up. Physically he was present, but mentally and emotionally he was absent. He didn't seem to care, nor did he truly comfort me throughout my contractions. He was on and off his phone, and my mother went in and out of the room in frustration with his actions. She didn't want him there and he didn't want her there. The tension in the room grew anytime they made eye contact. I had reached eight centimeters without an epidural. Physically, I was in excruciating pain. Emotionally, I was drained, and mentally, I was weak. The doctor came in to tell me my son's heart rate was declining. He said that if I continued to carry out a natural birth, I was going to face the great possibility of delivering a stillborn. My heart sank. All the fears I had from the experience with my first son came flooding in. I told him to prep me for a cesarean and I bawled. My mother consoled me, and Brent texted on his phone. When she stepped out of the room, Brent came over to hug me. I saw his arms wrapped around me, but I didn't feel any warmth in his touch.

Still, I allowed Brent to be the one to come with me into the operating room. Even though the situation was not ideal, and he didn't deserve to be there, I never wanted him to say I didn't give him the opportunity.

Our second son arrived without harm. I thanked God and all the medical staff. I was in love all over again and all the problems I had been dealing with didn't matter. My baby was here, and I could enjoy knowing he was safe. The first night, Brent helped me with feedings, diaper changes, and assisted me in getting off the bed so I could use the bathroom. The second day and night were different. He became annoyed when I would ask for help because he was tired and needed rest. I didn't entertain him, but I was upset with his lack of compassion. Anytime I had to use the restroom he would groan because he didn't want to hear the toilet flush or the sound of the faucet running. Still, I ignored him. He didn't look at our son the same way he looked at our oldest. He didn't have a connection with him, and our son preferred being held by me. Brent frequently left the room to walk around the hospital. It was apparent he didn't care to be there.

I allowed Brent to stay at the apartment to help with the adjustments. As naïve as I was, I thought it might do good for us to try and get a routine together to preserve our family. On our second night back from the hospital, we cried together as we discussed our feelings and wishes. Our oldest had a fever and I wasn't feeling too well. Brent said he would take care of all of us during the night. I desperately wanted to believe him, but I was skeptical. Even so, I gave him the opportunity to prove himself.

Every two hours he would have to get up to make a bottle. Our son cried off and on in between his feedings. This annoyed Brent and he screamed, "This isn't what I wanted! I'm never having sex with you again!"

I stared at him and said, "Well, you can always leave, and don't worry, because I don't find anything attractive about you anymore. Get away from my son!"

Brent shrugged his shoulders, rolled over, and went to sleep. I looked at him and thought to myself, *when are you going to muster up the courage to leave him for good?* I was so upset with myself for once again giving him another chance to disappoint me.

I woke up to the scent of Brent making breakfast. He apologized for his behavior, and I just nodded. His mother came over to pick him up because he left his work clothes at her house. Brent stated he needed to wash them before he went to work so he needed to leave earlier. As time would have it, as he and his mother were leaving, mine was arriving. My mother made it no secret she didn't care to see either of them. After he left, my mother stood before me and said, "He's off today. I spoke to his supervisor, and he said he doesn't work on Tuesdays. He's been lying to you and it's because he has a girlfriend."

I immediately said, "I know. I've known for a while; I just didn't want to focus on it."

My mother continued, "I didn't want to tell you because I didn't want anything to happen to you or the baby and for him to get custody of Aries. He's doing drugs and he's a threat to you and their safety. You need to get yourself and the baby checked, because his girlfriend is loose and they frequent the swinger's club."

I stood there nodding in agreement and my body filling up with rage. I stepped outside, made a phone call to a mutual acquaintance, and said, "Hey, I don't want you to feel dragged into this, but if you know, what is Brent's girlfriend's name?"

The response on the other line was quick. "I'm so glad you called. I have been wanting to tell you for so long, but I was scared something would happen to you and the new baby and I didn't want to interfere in your marriage. I don't know her name, but she shaves a portion of her hair and dyes it green."

I went on social media, took a screenshot of who I believed it was, and sent the person the image. "Yes, that's her." I thanked them and proceeded to text Brent and his mother.

I didn't have the greatest relationship with Brent's mother. It significantly dwindled over time, especially after Brent and I were married. There were countless times she disrespected me, made excuses for him, covered for him, and blamed me. A mother knows when their son is doing wrong and never once did she step in for the sake of my children's benefit. She was fully aware of his hanging out and drug use, and him not taking care of his responsibilities.

I sent the picture of the girlfriend to them and said, "I hope she's worth it. I know you're off today. You met her at Winds, hang out with her at Emperor, and go to Secrets." Winds and Emperor were both bars next to the restaurant he worked at. Secrets was the swingers club that was down the street from the apartment we once shared and coincidentally where the girlfriend worked. All his lies were exposed, and I was upset enough to start lashing out. I was made a fool time and time again, all while trying to preserve a false image of our family. The truth was that our marriage was broken beyond repair. It dawned on me that everyone knew exactly what he was doing, and because of it, I was truly embarrassed. It was one thing for immediate family and close friends to know what was going on, but for people around town to know? It was too much for me to bear. I couldn't handle all the feelings I had bottled up inside me: hurt, frustration, confusion, betrayal, anger, grief, self-pity, but the greatest was foolishness. It set off a war inside me. Me against myself. I knew better and I still gave him multiple chances to still prove me right! Why was I so stuck on him? Why was I so stuck on a marriage that clearly wasn't right? The pain surpassed my emotional understanding. I felt it on a physical level, and mentally I began to check out.

Brent made efforts to contact me. I ignored him completely. I was dev-astated. I felt like a zombie moving around to take care of our children and myself. My mother was quick to notice I was slipping into depression. "It's okay to feel what you're feeling, but don't let it run you," she told me. I needed to hear those words at that moment because shortly after, I received a message from Brent's cousin sending me pictures of what he posted. It was pictures of him enjoying himself at the swinger's club with his girlfriend. Looking at those images was like being gutted repeatedly. In each picture, the girlfriend's haircut was different, which told me their affair had been taking place for a lot longer than I thought. His cousin sent me a follow-up message cursing him and the girl out. She told me she loved me and the boys and no matter what, I would always be her cousin.

Angered by the pictures, I once again sent a text thread to Brent and his mother. It said, "Congratulations on losing your family. You don't have money to take care of your kids, but you have time and money to spend with this well-known drug user. Have a nice life. The boys and I deserve so much better. You should be so proud of yourself."

After I sent that text thread, I was on the receiving end of torment. Brent sent me messages to provoke a response. He was posting statuses and pic-tures inviting the cyber world into our lives. While he was busy attempting to provoke me, his actions provoked several online mutual friends and his family to take up arms on behalf of me and our boys. I received numerous messages from these individuals expressing their disgust with his behavior, advising me to rise above, encouraging me to give it to God, and asking what they could do to help. One person was adamant about me seeking a counselor because what Brent was doing was a form of abuse. There it was. The word abuse in black and white. I struggled with this word because he never physically hurt me. I always assumed abuse had to be physical. That's not always the case. I was fortunate enough that someone had seen through the smoke and called it what it was. I gathered my thoughts and began to move forward.

Three weeks had passed, and I scheduled a visitation for Brent and the boys. I was still upset with him and at the time of our meeting, I had also lost sensation in both of my legs from my thighs down to my feet. I made him aware, and he didn't seem to be phased. The visitation was cut short when he began boasting about his relationship and how I would like his girlfriend if I just gave her a chance. He had no issue adding insult to injury. I didn't want to hear any more of his abuse, so I instructed him to leave. We exchanged ugly words, and I didn't hear from him for five days. When I did hear from him again, it was a collect call. He was in jail.

I didn't say much at first. I just listened. He apologized for all he had put me through and said thank you. Confused, I asked, "Thank you?"

"Yes, I know you knew there was a warrant out for my arrest and that I was arrested not long after I left the apartment."

I told him he was arrested because of whatever it was that he did. He said, "Well, I know it was you who spoke to my PO and because of that, they issued a warrant."

I fired back, "You had a warrant out because YOU failed the drug test. Whether I spoke to your probation officer or not, you were using. That's all your doing."

He sweetly replied, "I know, and I didn't call to fight. I just wanted to thank you and tell you I love you and I am so sorry for the hell I put you through. If you're comfortable with it, could we please talk during a visit, or could you at least answer the phone? I want to make things right."

I should have said no, but I said, "We'll see." After that, he made daily calls.

Our wedding anniversary came, and two of my cousins and my best friend Natalie took me to dinner, so I wouldn't be alone. I put on as good a front as I could, but inside I was hurting thinking about what Brent did the previous year. My life was completely upside down, and I had no idea just how much crazier things were going to get. As predicted, he called while I was at dinner, and I answered. His tone instantly changed when he heard Natalie's fiancé order everyone a drink. "How come you never want to go drinking with me?"

"I've been pregnant for the last two years. Why would I go drinking? You never made plans to take me anywhere because you were too busy going places with other women!" I replied.

"Yeah, I guess you're right, but why are you out? You just gave birth a month ago. Who is watching the boys? That's irresponsible of you."

He pissed me off, and I hung up on him. He called back and I answered. "Brent, we're not doing this. When you call, it's going to strictly be to talk to the boys."

He reeled me in and said, "Did you just hang up on me? Are you serious? You want to know how many girls there were? Ask me whatever you want, and I'll tell you. You want to know? There were four: Anna, Eve, Lisa, and Dimarie."

I scoffed and said, "I knew you slept with Anna!"

He cut me off. "I didn't say I slept with her, I just said there were four girls I was talking to, and I've only been with one of them."

We went back and forth for a few minutes. I brought up all the evidence I had against him. "You are using drugs and you use it with your girlfriend! That's why you never come around on Tuesday nights because you go to the swinger's club with her, and those nights are known to be a white out. You've been doing cocaine!" He cut me off and said, "I stopped doing cocaine. I've been doing Adderall."

DING! DING! DING! I had my answer. A specific one at that, and it was recorded on a jail call! Finally, he came clean about what he was using.

My intuition was right and lucky for me, he was upset enough to say it. His pride was hurt that I was the one out enjoying myself while he had to sit still. I was elated that I would be able to obtain that call should I need it in the future.

When our call ended, I went inside to share the news. Everyone was glad I had an official answer and we celebrated. I didn't hear from Brent for four days. I shouldn't have answered any additional calls, but I did, so he could hear the kids. Once again, he apologized for his behavior and said he was just upset that I went out on our anniversary. I laughed and said, "You have a girlfriend, and you were upset I went out on our anniversary? If you were out, you would have been spending our anniversary with her!" He was quiet then proceeded to start with his usual lies. I cut him short and said I had to go. As the days passed, I continued to lose sensation throughout my body. I knew I was walking but couldn't feel it. I became frustrated, and during a call with Brent, I broke down. I blamed all our problems on him. I blamed him for not being the man he vowed to be. I blamed him for choosing a lifestyle not suitable for a family. I blamed him for me repeatedly questioning my intuition to give him the benefit of the doubt. I blamed him for selling me a dream he was never going to make a reality. And the list continued. I cried, stating I had no idea what was going on with my body and I didn't have a husband to help me get through this. I complained about how unfair everything was and how he didn't care about anyone but himself. Brent cried with me. He promised he was going to fix all the wrongs he had done. He vowed there wouldn't be any more girlfriends or friends that ran in bad circles. He promised change and he would be the husband I deserved and the father our boys deserved. He made promise after promise.

That night I remember praying for change. I wanted so badly for our lives to make a turn for the better. I wanted God to use our mess and bring us closer than before. I wanted to be able to forgive him and not bring up what he had done anymore. I wanted him to be a man of his word. I wanted him to choose me and our boys. I wanted him to give himself to God and be done with drugs once and for all. I wanted the impossible to be possible.

Christmas was approaching, and Brent was still in jail. He became frustrated about still being incarcerated for a violation of probation charge, while I was dealing with my own frustrations. I had lost sensation in my body from my neck down. My hands up to my elbows were constantly burning and my fingers were locking. I couldn't change our children's diapers, I couldn't make or hold their bottles, and I couldn't bathe them. My body was shutting down. By then, I was staying at my parents' house for the help I needed.

Meanwhile, Brent and I were communicating better than we had in months. We extensively discussed him going to therapy, looking into rehabilitation, and joining NA. We talked about studying the Bible together and going to marriage counseling. He was concerned about my health and continued with his promises. Every other day I received a letter in the mail from him. Despite his knowledge of the decline in my physical abilities, he still requested that I write back as often as I was receiving his letters. In fact, he begged me. He said seeing my letters come in the mail made him temporarily escape from his reality. The urgency in his voice pushed me to give in to his wishes. I answered his calls multiple times a day and struggled to reply to the letters he sent. My credit card usage was increasing to maintain our phone communication. I was slipping further into debt to accommodate his desires when he wasn't doing anything but feeding me words. I reminded him of his promises and that the real test would be once he got out.

Brent could promise whatever he wanted—all day—while he was locked up, but once he obtained his freedom, he would have to work to show the change in his character. He had failed so many times before, and I suppressed my gut feeling that he was going to mess up again. I didn't want to deal with it, especially when there was more on my plate than I could handle, and I was scared. The familiarity of his voice gave me comfort and took me back to the times when he cared about me. I desperately wanted a miracle, but I was afraid of being alone. It didn't occur to me that I was already alone. He had neglected me time and time again in the most vulnerable moments, and I knew he would do it again the second he became upset with me. It was in his nature, and I was hopeful for something I knew wasn't going to happen. I was so brainwashed, as many of us become. The longer we stay in a situation that does not serve us, the more we devalue our worth and settle for less than what we truly deserve.

I didn't realize that what I was going through could be labeled as abuse. I had a very narrow definition of abuse, and since I hadn't experienced that, I didn't think I could be a victim. I'm grateful that I confided in a trusted friend who helped me see that what I had been going through did indeed qualify as abuse. Sometimes, when you're deep in the struggle just trying to get by, it's hard to see your situation clearly. It's crucial to open up to others and God about the pain you're going through—whether it's emotional, mental, spiritual, or physical—so you can start the healing process. Only by acknowledging the depths of our pain can we begin that journey to healing.

Psalm 147:3 (NIV) says "He heals the brokenhearted and binds up their wounds." When we deny the hurt we've experienced and/or minimize it or blame ourselves for it, we aren't opening ourselves up to the healing that God promises us. When we come to Him with honesty, our broken hearts, our weakness, and the wounds we've accrued from the person or people who have hurt us, then we will no longer have to pretend we have everything under control. We can rest in Him and the knowledge that He is looking out for us. God can and will restore us wholly and completely.

After you have uncovered the red flags, it can be daunting to figure out your next course of action. Despite all the hardships your loved one caused, the idea of parting ways may be unbearable. Though you may feel weak, you are in the perfect position for God to reveal His strength. For nothing is impossible for Him. God will help you shift your focus to prioritizing your safety. Be patient with yourself and take things one day at a time. The needs of the drug abuser can no longer come before your own. You cannot continue to live according to their rules and selfish desires. The time for change is now.

Part II

Prioritize Your Safety

Chapter Eight

Setting Boundaries

H olding onto the hope that your loved one will recover is a crucial aspect of supporting them through addiction. However, there may come a point when staying with them jeopardizes your safety and hinders your ability to lead a healthy life, especially for your children. Prioritizing your safety might initially feel selfish and challenging, but it is not; it's protective, healthy, and necessary. The first step in prioritizing your safety is establishing clear boundaries. Being firm and resolute in these boundaries is essential for them to be effective. Explicit boundaries may be the key to finding peace in your life again. I learned this the hard way.

Two days before the new year, I found myself in the hospital, scheduled for an MRI of my brain and spinal cord to uncover the mystery of my health issues. After getting the results from the MRI, I was diagnosed with multiple sclerosis. An incurable but treatable condition. Examining at the images, I noticed several lesions on my brain. The weight of this diagnosis hit me, and I started thinking about the challenges I might face in life and how it would impact my children.

Questions flooded my mind. Would Brent be my support through this? Was he ready to fulfill his vows, taking care of me in sickness and health? Would this be the ultimate test of our marriage? When I shared the news with him over the phone, I waited for his response. I could hear the struggle in his voice as he fought back tears, intermittently clearing his throat. He reassured me, claiming I was the strongest person he knew and that he would stand by me through every challenge this disease presented. Once again, I gave him the benefit of the doubt.

The day Brent was released, I had been home from the hospital for less than two weeks. While I had regained a significant amount of sensation in my body, my hands still faced some challenges in full functionality. The burning sensation in my arms had subsided, but my fingertips remained numb. When he came back to the apartment, we spent time playing with our sons and had dinner together. After putting our boys to sleep, Brent held my hands and observed the difficulties with the movement of my fingers. Genuine concern filled his eyes, and tears welled up. Trying to hold back my own tears, I told him I needed him to follow through on everything we had discussed. I shared my fears, and he reassured me that he would do everything he had promised.

The first three days and nights after he was released from jail, Brent was very helpful. He cooked, he cleaned, he changed diapers, fed our boys, and helped me bathe them. He got up during the night when our sons cried and took care of them. I was so grateful that he did what he said he would. I worked long hours, so the nighttime help I received allowed me to rest. Though I was getting comfortable, my was guard up.

The fourth night took an expected turn. After Brent had bathed our boys, I spoke to him about studying the Bible and reading a couple's book together. He wasn't interested in either. His eyes were glued to the television. I asked if he had looked into therapy, NA, or marriage counseling, and his answer was no. He didn't think it was necessary at the time because things were going well. I felt an emotional blow. Here we were again, I thought. Nothing was going to change. He had plenty of time on his hands, still jobless and not putting in the effort to fulfill the plans we had discussed while he was in jail. He fed me a string of empty promises, and once more, I fell for his deceit. I couldn't even be angry with him. I knew better, but I wanted to believe in the fairy tale he painted. I was exhausted from this repetitive cycle. I turned off the television and asked, "Do you even want to be married?"

He looked at me and said, "I don't know."

I rolled my eyes, shook my head, and told him I was going to bed.

That night our boys woke up in the middle of the night. The first time, Brent tended to their needs. I listened and watched just as I had before. The second time, he didn't move so I asked him to check on the children, and he responded, "I've been doing it every night while you've been getting rest. It's my turn to get some rest." With that, he rolled over. After tending to our children's needs, I informed him that he would need to leave in the morning. He simply said, "Okay," and went back to sleep. It didn't surprise me. He wasn't cut out to be a supportive husband or father. I knew this was the end. Our relationship wouldn't progress any further. It only took four days for his selfish behavior to resurface, following the same patterns. Despite the pain, I was prepared to move forward. I deserved better, and more importantly, our children deserved better.

The following day, he went to his parents' house. I dropped off our boys at my parents' place and headed to work. About halfway into my shift, I received a call informing me that both of our sons were unwell. One had a high fever, and the other was dealing with diarrhea and wasn't eating. I reached out to their doctor to schedule an appointment, but the earliest slot available was on Tuesday. It was only Friday. I left work and called Brent, explaining the situation and my plan to take them to the ER at the children's hospital for immediate attention. I offered to pick him up so he could come along. However, he started making excuses about being up all night and needing rest. I told him it was selfish of him to prioritize rest when our children needed him. "They're babies and your sleep is not more important than them receiving the care they need! What is wrong with you?" He groaned and said he was getting dressed and asked me to pick him up. Once I had both children in the car, I headed to his parents' house. He got in the car and complained about us going to the ER instead of to their doctor.

"Did you not hear anything I said about their doctor not having any openings until Tuesday?" I asked. "It's Friday. They're sick today. They need to be seen today."

Still, he continued with his complaining. The entire car ride was filled with his disapproval of us going to the ER. He complained under his breath, in the waiting room, and continued to complain once we were in the patient room.

"You are so selfish!" I told him. "This is about our boys, and you can't get past your desire to sleep? And you wonder why I don't trust you to be alone with them! Don't worry. Once we leave, I'll take you back to your mom's and you can sleep the rest of the day and night away. I'll take care of our boys. At least they have one parent who will."

Brent didn't seem phased at all.

The car ride was quiet, with Brent engrossed in texting on his phone. He mentioned using his mother's car to come over the next day. I looked at him and remarked, "I didn't expect anything else. I mean, you left me to care for a sick one-year-old and a newborn just four days after I had a c-section. And now, you're doing it again. You seem to have an issue with helping take care of anyone but yourself."

He shot me a dirty look. But when I pulled into his parents' driveway, he attempted to sweet-talk me, suggesting that we needed a night away from each other to get back on track. I shook my head and firmly stated,

"No, you're done playing mind games with me. We'll see you for a visit tomorrow." I put the car in reverse and left. The constant texting in the car triggered my intuition. I sensed he might be back in touch with his old friends, possibly even his girlfriend. It seemed like he was heading towards using again, and his behaviors indicated he was getting the itch. I had to be extra cautious.

Living through days filled with tension and constantly wondering if Brent was clean wasn't the life I wanted for myself or what I wanted our children to consider as normal. I reached a point where I had enough and established the rules that should have been in place a long time ago. I explicitly outlined my expectations for a marriage and informed him that if he couldn't meet those expectations, then we needed to initiate the divorce process.

One night, I called him to come over as we had discussed. My hands were locking up, and the boys needed a bath. He claimed he didn't know if he could make it because he didn't have access to a car. I suggested he tell his mom that he needed to do something for the boys and would be right back, emphasizing it was for the grandkids she claimed to love so much. He asked me not to make smart remarks and said he would ask her and call me back. When he did, he fed me the same line—no access to his mom's car. I responded, "Not surprised in the least," and hung up on him. I sought help from my neighbor, and she stayed with me throughout the night. I sensed something was off; it was a Tuesday night, his infamous hangout night at the swinger's club. I knew he was lying about not being able to help due to circumstances. It was a deliberate lie, as he had other plans he deemed more important than his responsibilities as a father. I asked a friend to let me know if Brent passed by the restaurant where he used to work. The following afternoon, I received a picture of him sitting at the bar, drinking with his girlfriend.

Brent came over the following night. He was dressed up and wore cologne. I was annoyed, witnessing him tell the boys how much he loved them. I was even more annoyed when he said he wasn't going to be able to visit with them for long because he had to go to work. He had gotten a job at the same bar he was hanging out at. I interrupted him and said, "You can't love them that much if you have time to go to the bar instead of giving them a bath." His face reddened, exposing his underlying embarrassment. The enthusiasm in his voice disappeared, and he avoided making eye contact with me.

"What are you talking about?"

I snapped back, "I know you were at the bar yesterday with your girlfriend so all that talk about you not having a ride and you were going to be stuck in the house was a lie. You're using again. It makes sense because your actions aren't that of a real father. You're a social media dad! Just like your mom is a social media grandma." The more I spoke the more upset I got. "You know what, just leave. How dare you pick anything over our children. You act like you care, but you give them less than the bare minimum. You're not a man, and I'll be damned if our boys learn to be anything like you. You're going to be sorry when you see them calling some other man dad. They deserve so much better! Get out!"

It felt like chains were breaking off me. He tried to make me feel sorry for him, saying, "Baby, please don't do this," accompanied by sad faces—the kind I used to fall for. However, this time, I wasn't budging. I could see from his actions that he was going to be the type of father who came and went as he pleased in our children's lives. The anticipation of my children being let down in the future consumed my thoughts. I already didn't trust him to be alone with them; what if he used substances or left something hazardous around and they got their hands on it? What if he was too preoccupied resting and slept through their basic needs? His choice of associates raised concerns, and what if they did something harmful to my children or witnessed him doing something and covered for him? It was time to break the cycle.

"The next time you hear from me will be through my lawyer. Don't call me, text me, or show up. You're not welcome here anymore." I was serious. Not to mention hurt, angry, and felt so guilty for picking him as my husband and father of my children. All of this could have been avoided if I would have asked God if this was truly the man for me. Now, I had a whole drama series in my home.

Brent left and tried calling and texting me. I sent one long text message telling him he was not welcome to come over and the reasons why. I was very specific about his drug use and that it was not suitable to have around our children. I blocked his number, all of his social media accounts, and began looking into getting an attorney.

One week later, Brent unexpectedly showed up at the house. I opened the door to tell him he wasn't welcome and to reread the last message I sent. He begged to see the boys. I told him to provide me with a clean drug test. If he wasn't willing to do that, I wasn't willing to let him see the boys. I closed the door in his face. He kept knocking for a few minutes until he left. I stood my ground. Brent showed up again a week later. He was teary-eyed and begged to see our boys. I asked for his drug test results. He said he was done with everything: he was clean, he wasn't hanging out downtown anymore, and he wasn't dating his girlfriend. He asked if we could talk. I stepped outside and closed the door behind me, put out my hand, and said, "So show me the proof. No drug test, no visitations."

I turned to go back inside and that's when Brent lost it. He pushed the door open from behind me. I placed my right hand on the doorknob and immediately swung my left arm out to the side to block him from going inside. He pushed against me, forcing his way in. I yelled for him to stop and to leave. He disregarded my demands. I struggled to turn and face him and when I did, his eyes were so dilated, I couldn't recognize him. He continued to push against me, and I stumbled multiple times. Had it not been for the countertop to my side, I would have fallen over. My body was in a weakened state. I wasn't able to fight back like I wanted to. My hands were tingling and locking up and I was fearful that if he hit my stomach, I would have an injury to my cesarean wound which wasn't fully healed. Our oldest was right behind me holding his blanket to his face, screaming and crying. I begged Brent to stop. "It's okay. Daddy's here," he told our son. I tried one last time to push him back, but he overpowered me, pushed past my arms, and grabbed our son.

Aries cried hysterically and reached out for me. I grabbed him from Brent. I did my best to comfort him and kept telling Brent he needed to leave. He stood by the front door and refused. My heart was racing, and the room spinning. Brent had never done this before, and he did this in front of our children. I couldn't organize my thoughts. I watched Brent and our three-month-old in the playpen while I comforted our one-year-old who was upset by what he just witnessed and uncomfortable because he needed a diaper change. This was like something out of a Lifetime movie. Brent wore an evil grin as he looked back at me. "I'm going to tell you one last time to leave or I'm going to have the police remove you," I told him.

Without hesitation, Brent replied, "Call the cops because I'm not leaving."

I knew things were going to turn ugly, and I was braced for the storm. I called the police, and throughout the entire process, Brent mocked me. He sat on the floor at the junction of the tile and carpet, saying to our 3-month-old, "It's okay. Daddy is done with probation. I might get arrested, but that's okay because you're worth it. Mommy and Daddy are still married, and Daddy can be here." He was entirely delusional, smiling at our baby. I tried to listen to the phone operator and Brent simultaneously while standing guard for my safety and the safety of our children. I wasn't sure what else he might do. My mind was scattered, and I did not feel safe with him there.

Shortly after I ended the call, the police were banging on the front door. Brent casually got up from the floor and answered the door. He was taken outside, and the officers came in to speak with me. I explained why we were separated, highlighting that his name was not on the lease. I mentioned that none of his belongings were in the apartment, and he was not invited over. I told them about him pushing his way through me to enter, emphasizing that I had been hospitalized a few weeks prior for my MS. They noticed the locking of my hands and fingers, and I informed them about my recent cesarean, explaining that I hadn't fully healed. They requested a statement and asked if I wanted to press charges. I said yes, providing his probation officer's name, as he was on probation. Despite feeling distraught, I was determined not to back down this time. I had endured more than my fair share of mistreatment from Brent, but this incident was the final straw. If he could do this while I was vulnerable in front of the children, he was capable of worse. Witnessing my baby distressed and hearing his screams were compelling reasons to put an end to this madness. The cycle had to stop, and there couldn't be a next time. I knew the road ahead would be challenging, but I understood that traversing it was necessary to create a healthy and safe environment for my children and me.

Setting new boundaries in a relationship with a drug abuser can be very difficult, but to prioritize your safety it is necessary. They will most likely not respond well and be very hurt by your clearly defined boundaries after they've been able to take advantage of you for so long, but it is absolutely vital that you hold your ground, no matter how much they are hurting. In their book *Boundaries*, Dr. Henry Cloud and Dr. Alex Townsend wrote:

When we begin to set boundaries with people we love, a really hard thing happens: they hurt. They may feel a hole where you used to plug up their aloneness, their disorganization, or their financial irresponsibility. Whatever it is, they will feel a loss. If you love them, this will be difficult for you to watch. But, when you are dealing with someone who is hurting, remember that your boundaries are both necessary for you and helpful for them. If you have been enabling them to be irresponsible, your limit setting may nudge them toward responsibility.[1]

You can't continue to take responsibility for their emotions and reactions. You can only take responsibility for your actions and your needs, and you have to stand up for yourself because your loved one suffering from addiction will continue to take advantage of you if you don't.

After you've gotten some practice in setting boundaries, you will begin to confidently say no and not feel bad about it. I recently found out that "no" is a complete sentence. You can say no to somebody and not have to explain yourself. Again, this goes back to learning and finding out who will respect your boundaries, who will respect you as a person, and who will respect your healing journey.

In Galatians 6:7-10 (MSG), the Apostle Paul writes, "What a person plants, he will harvest. The person who plants selfishness, ignoring the needs of others—ignoring God!—harvests a crop of weeds. All he'll have to show for his life is weeds! But the one who plants in response to God, letting God's Spirit do the growth work in him, harvests a crop of real life, eternal life. So let's not allow ourselves to get fatigued doing good. At the right time we will harvest a good crop if we don't give up, or quit."

When you plant boundaries, you will reap healthier relationships. When you make it known that you won't be taken advantage of anymore, you'll reap clarity. By working with God to set the boundaries that you need in your life, you will begin creating and building a life that will lead to more health, joy, peace, and fulfillment. By setting boundaries, you are taking the first step toward your own safety.

---

1. Cloud, Henry, and John Sims Townsend. *Boundaries: When to Say Yes, How to Say No to Take Control of Your Life*. Grand Rapids, MI: Zondervan, 2017.

Chapter Nine

The Journey to Healing

Only by confiding in the people I trusted could I continue the process of prioritizing my safety and that of my kids. It's easy to become entangled in the reality and lies woven by a drug abuser, leading us to deny our own experiences and feelings. There are often numerous fears that prevent us from opening up, and these fears can be simultaneous and contradictory:

1) What if it's not as bad as I think, and I'm just overreacting?

2) What if it is that bad, and I have to leave a relationship I've poured my heart and soul into?

3) What if they no longer want to be my friend because of the problems I'm facing?

4) What if they perceive me as the problem?

These concerns can easily hinder you from seeking the help you desperately need. Opening up and trusting others can be challenging after enduring betrayal from your loved one multiple times, but it is a crucial step to ensure your safety and well-being.

When the police officers came to my house, they provided me with the case number and information for the local domestic violence shelter. They said they would be in contact and that it was important for me to protect myself and my children. I nodded in agreement and thanked them for their service. After they left, I took a deep breath and called my mother, and she showed up just as fast as the police had. I explained what happened and that this was the ultimate wake-up call. I dealt with plenty of emotional, mental, and verbal abuse and it just turned physical. He didn't mark up my face, and I am fortunate for that, but it doesn't excuse him for what he did. Physical abuse starts somewhere. He had no problem dominating me when I was at my weakest. I didn't want to find out what he could do if given another opportunity.

Feeling unsafe and uneasy in the apartment, I began packing clothes for myself and the boys to stay at my parents' house. There was a knock on the door. One of the police officers had returned to check on me, mentioning a call I had missed containing further information I needed. He brought up something about the car Brent had driven over, sparking my curiosity. I descended the stairs to check if I recognized the vehicle. Although it was unfamiliar, I took a picture of the license plate and front end, thinking that if I ever drove around or parked somewhere, I wanted to know if that car was following me. I didn't trust any of the people Brent surrounded himself with and this had to have been someone I never met. I couldn't trust them, just like I couldn't trust him.

While I was talking to the officer, Brent attempted to call me. The officer advised against taking any of his calls, emphasizing that I did the right thing and that abusers often blame the victims. He assured me that by not engaging with him, he couldn't get into my head. After the officer left, my mother and I gathered our bags and my children. As we descended the stairs, we noticed someone getting into the car Brent had driven over. I stopped and stared at the man; I had no clue who he was. I memorized his face, pondering how many times Brent had used a car from someone

I didn't know or how many different individuals had dropped him off here. How many people, unfamiliar to me, knew where I lived? Were these people using like Brent? Were they involved in selling? Did he owe them anything? Concerned, I told my mother, "I have to leave this apartment. It's not safe. In the worst-case scenario, if he owes someone something and they want to cause harm, they could go after family members. My children's lives could be at stake! How could I have not thought about this?" My mom tried to comfort me by assuring me it was because I was blinded by love, but the good thing was, I was thinking more clearly now.

The journey to recovery began.

Although I anticipated a challenging process, I was committed to going the distance to secure a brighter future for myself and my boys. My goal was to offer them a strong foundation of good morals and a genuine understanding of right and wrong, breaking free from the toxic cycle of generational curses. I reached a pivotal moment where I needed to deepen my faith and fully surrender to God. Previously lukewarm and relying on my own strength, I realized the significance of seeking God wholeheartedly. Reflecting on Revelation 3:15-16 (ESV), "I know your works: you are neither cold nor hot. Would that you were either cold or hot! So, because you are lukewarm, and neither hot nor cold, I will spit you out of my mouth." I recognized the need for a complete surrender. Believing that staying in a toxic environment had contributed to my declining physical health, I acknowledged that my stubbornness and resistance to seeking God's guidance had taken a toll. I understood that my physical breakdown was a sign that the situation was beyond my control, and I needed to let go. Embracing the idea that God's strength is perfected in our weakness, I adopted a habit of praying and seeking God's help in difficult times, praising Him in moments of joy and sorrow. I decided to release situations I didn't understand to God rather than seeking answers on my own. I had chosen to fully align with God, embracing the Scripture from Proverbs 3:5-6 (NIV), "Trust in the Lord with all your heart and lean not on your own understanding; in all your ways submit to Him and He will make your paths straight." I recognized that we are not meant to know everything or fix everyone but to build our lives on the solid foundation of God's Word.

I had to separate myself from what I wanted in my life and invite in what God wanted in my life. He wanted me to put Him first—seeking Him first before seeking counsel from anyone else. He wanted me to trust Him in all areas of my life and didn't want me hurting and constantly in pain. He doesn't want you there either. He wants us to build a community that glorifies His love for us. He can't be glorified if we are settling for chaos and wanting what our flesh wants.

I prayed and thanked God for everything I had in my life. There were blessings all around me that I was not giving much attention to. I had family and friends who genuinely loved me and my children and had our best interests at heart. I spent entirely too much time and energy on wanting to receive fulfillment from a spouse who was never meant to be my spouse. I had fallen victim to the lies of the enemy. Every time I went against my gut feeling, I placed myself and more importantly, I placed my children's lives in an environment that was not going to bear good fruit. I turned to God, seeking help and making a commitment to obedience. I asked Him to transform my life and turn the challenging experiences I went through into something good. Following His guidance, I reached out to the domestic violence organization recommended by the officer and started receiving counseling to address the trauma I had faced.

This organization played a crucial role in reshaping my mindset. It provided a haven where I could express my thoughts and emotions without fear of judgment. The counselors, all of whom had experienced some form of domestic violence, empathized with the tactics of abusers. They had overcome their own abuse and were eager to share their insights, offering unbiased perspectives. During many sessions, I shed tears as I released my frustrations about the profound betrayal I endured, the anger directed towards Brent, the influence of drugs, myself, and others involved. This cathartic process was pivotal in paving the way for my healing.

My vulnerability to constructive ideas became a gateway to self-improvement, aligning myself with the woman I aspired to be and, more importantly, the woman God intended me to become. Armed with new-found knowledge, I initiated the process of shedding broken pieces that were not meant to accompany me on my journey. The counselors assigned exercises that prompted me to view situations from alternative perspectives. Some shared relevant scripture, while others sent weekly motivational quotes. I was encouraged to replace television time with reading books, fostering a positive mental environment essential for working through and overcoming my pain.

The domestic violence organization also helped me with legal counsel. I was given step-by-step instructions for filing an order of protection, given representation for the court proceedings I encountered, answers to any legal questions I had, and assistance with filing for divorce. The lawyer I worked with was sharp, easily accessible, and willing to go the extra mile to provide the best service. Because of her diligence, I was able to obtain the recorded jail call with Brent admitting to his drug use and provide it to my divorce attorney.

I incorporated the habit of reading daily devotionals at the beginning of my day. I invested in books authored by individuals who openly expressed their belief in God, particularly in Jesus Christ, sharing the wisdom they gained by trusting in God during their personal storms. I delved into reading the Bible independently, working through a study guide. Regular church attendance became a part of my routine, supplemented by watching sermons online on various days. I replaced my usual music with worship tunes, creating an environment conducive to allowing God to move freely. These adjustments not only elevated my mood and improved my relationships but also paved the way for the right individuals to enter my life. Tuning out negative thoughts, talk, and individuals I didn't need around me or my children became easier. Focusing on God resulted in blessings pouring out at a pace that was almost overwhelming—and over-whelmingly joyful. Every step I took in faith released another blessing.

I had an injunction against Brent and stood firm in court when he tried to reconcile. A part of me wanted to believe what he said, but after everything I had gone through and the countless times I had given him a chance, I knew this time was no different. He placed the blame on me for being incarcerated instead of taking ownership of his actions. Seeing him in handcuffs and a jumpsuit broke my heart, especially when he could have made a better choice. The silence I received from the non-contact order gave me the strength to keep pushing toward true freedom from the merry-go-round relationship we had. It brought stability into my life, and it showed me how much better off I was without him.

The journey of healing requires patience and self-kindness, especially when feelings of grief resurface. On those challenging days, I leaned even harder into my faith in God. While it wasn't always easy, it proved to be the right course of action. I sought positive outlets to process my emotions, implementing changes in my diet and incorporating exercise. Guided by God and the supportive community around me, I discovered a restoration surpassing my pre-broken state. Multiple reasons to smile emerged, and the assurance of God blessing me double for my suffering brought comfort.

I reminded myself that time is constant and irreplaceable, prompting me to focus less on unraveling my ex-husband's actions and more on the promises I made to myself at the altar. Instead of dwelling on the reality of the situation, I shifted my thoughts toward what I truly deserved and envisioned the life I wanted, affirming its attainability.

Healing requires that we shift our mindset and let go of narratives we've continually believed. Narratives like: If you're not there for them, who will be? How could I leave when I committed to them for life? Or I just need to be patient and keep suffering for a bit; it will pay off; they will change.

These narratives kept me stuck in an abusive situation that was harming me and my children—physically and emotionally. I needed new narratives that would promote health and safety for my family. Narratives like: By putting your needs first and setting healthy boundaries, you are setting a good example for your children. By no longer letting yourself be taken advantage of you can put more energy toward the needs and desires of your children and yourself. Creating a loving environment for your children is so important for their development.

When old narratives try to sneak in again, that is when you need to open up to other people about what you are experiencing and allow them to speak the truth and reality of the situation. Sometimes you need them to help you establish the narratives that will aid you in your healing. My parents, my best friend Natalie, and the counselors at the domestic violence shelter did this for me throughout my relationship and separation from Brent. They were guides on my healing journey, and I'm so thankful for them.

Hebrews 10:24-25 (NIV) says, "And let us consider how we may spur one another on toward love and good deeds, not giving up meeting together, as some are in the habit of doing, but encouraging one another—and all the more as you see the Day approaching." This is what a good community does for you. They encourage you and support you through hard times. They meet with you, and they point you toward God. This is what my people did for me during this season in my life.

Who are those people in your life? The people who don't judge you and let you be you. People that you feel safe with and can make you laugh and lift you up when you need it the most. People who you reach out to about the little things throughout your day or the big things that you want to celebrate. It's a rare thing that you find people that you're that comfortable with. For some of us, it takes a lot for us to open up or to get close to anyone, so when you find that kind of friendship or relationship, value it and hold it close.

Chapter Ten
Changing the Narrative

I cannot be held accountable for the choices my ex-husband made, but I take responsibility for the choices I made. Disregarding the red flags, which were God's warnings, contributed significantly to my heartache. Throughout my relationship with Brent, I frequently downplayed or dismissed my intuition to cling to something that ultimately harmed me. In relationships with drug abusers, manipulators, or abusers, their deceitful actions can leave our intuition in disarray. It becomes a dilemma of trusting someone we've trusted for years versus our gut feeling, which may be signaling otherwise. Our intuition, the inner voice, becomes more pronounced when we heed its guidance and fades when we ignore it.

Our intuition is a gift from God that we tend to disregard for the sake of our fleshly desires. Our fleshly desires and God's will are not always the same. It is imperative to pray that the desires of our hearts align with His will and His plan for our lives. If we do not regularly consult Him with our plans, we can veer off course and cause our turmoil. Being rooted in God's Word will build the solid foundation we need for our lives. When this is established, our vision is clearer, and we will make better choices. We won't accept the mediocre. We won't normalize what culture wants us to normalize. We won't make excuses to stay where we are not meant to stay.

We won't try to fix situations beyond our control. We won't entertain foolishness. We won't give countless opportunities to those who continuously hurt us all for the sake of "love." We won't discredit the gift of intuition and we will find comfort in not knowing everything. We will know when to walk away from people or situations that only take from us and don't pour back into us. We will know our value. We will see ourselves through God's eyes. We will set a standard and demand to be treated with respect. We will know what real love truly is.

During the six years of trying to build a life with Brent, I continuously set my intuition and better judgment aside to try to be there for him in the ways I thought I needed to. To trust him unquestionably, to work through any conflicts that arose, and to protect him even at the risk of my own safety. Going against my gut feeling and what I felt God was speaking to me sent me down a very dark and lonely path. I was doing the best I could at the time, and it's taken time for me to realize and accept that. Through this experience, I have learned how important it is to trust your judgment and your instincts, because nine times out of ten, it will lead you to truth and freedom. If something doesn't sit right in you, then it probably isn't right. Explore, investigate, and follow that feeling.

Once you've ignored that voice inside you for a length of time, it seems to diminish, fading to a point where it becomes almost inaudible. Amidst the flood of thoughts, emotions, and deceitful narratives spun by your loved one, you grapple with trying to unravel the web of lies they've woven around you. However, the inner voice never completely vanishes, and the more you heed its guidance, the more pronounced it becomes.

In *Bird by Bird*, Anne Lamott shares her insights into how to revive your better judgment, "You get your intuition back when you make space for it, when you stop the chattering of the rational mind. The rational mind doesn't nourish you. You assume that it gives you the truth, because the rational mind is the golden calf that this culture worships, but this is not true. Rationality squeezes out much that is rich and juicy and fascinating." [1] Make space for your intuition. I ignored my intuition and waited for cold hard evidence regarding my suspicions. But I should have made more space for my intuition and let it lead me toward taking healthy steps for myself. I believe that God was trying to show me what path to take, but I kept following my heart instead of His Spirit.

After my separation from Brent, I was free from all the bondages once attached to me. I walked with relaxed shoulders and my head held high. I started feeling more confident in myself and my choices.

Once the injunction and non-contact order were removed, Brent and I had to find a way to co-parent. It was like climbing up a steep mountain in the rain. It was difficult to be around him without all the memories resurfacing, but I always prayed before we met up at a public location to ensure my judgment wouldn't become clouded. My prayers worked because all I saw when I looked at him was a giant red flag and when he spoke, I saw the red flag waving.

Often, he questioned why I wouldn't let him take our boys anywhere without me present. I gave the same two answers every time, "I don't trust you" and "If you're not using drugs, I know your girlfriend is, and that lifestyle is not welcome around our boys." He would dance around with his words, giving me all sorts of excuses claiming he had changed, that he was not using any drugs, and that his girlfriend wouldn't be around our boys. While lacking solid proof, I knew he was lying, and this time around, I chose to stick to my intuition. I knew that it would only be a matter of time before I had a definitive answer. I trusted that God would provide that to me right when it was needed. And He did.

The old days of putting what's best for me aside, just to make sure someone else is okay or sugarcoating the truth for someone else, were over.

It was important to establish a season of me pouring into myself. I had spent so many years of my life pouring into and giving to everyone else, sometimes to the wrong people. It's draining when you pour into what's not supposed to be in your life, because it's one-sided. I lost my voice throughout the process of giving so much of myself to other people, specifically my ex-husband. And I ended up somewhere that I didn't belong, putting up with things that I shouldn't have been putting up with.

Upon reaching this juncture, introspection becomes imperative. I had to confront, or at least acknowledge, that the issue wasn't external; it was within myself. I questioned why I allowed such situations, why my self-worth plummeted to a point where I accepted toxicity, and why I believed I deserved such circumstances. Initiating this self-examination journey led me to rediscover myself, reclaim my voice, and exercise better judgment. Rebuilding trust in myself and my intuition was a slow process, yet the rewards were so worth it.

I've come a long way from the abuse, toxicity, and being taken advantage of. Establishing boundaries and selectively opening up to trustworthy friends and advocates became crucial in protecting my voice from belittlement. If these boundaries mean remaining single for a while, that's perfectly fine. I've learned to relish my own company and, in the process, discovered a newfound love and appreciation for myself. Happiness has become intrinsic, and I now recognize the value I bring to any relationship. The ultimate goal is to enjoy one's own company, being content with who you are until you find those who genuinely appreciate and understand you. When the time comes to love again, I aim to be joyfully married, not just content in marriage. My desire is for a healthy union with the spouse God has destined for me.

There's just no room for me to accept anything less than what I deserve. I have embraced who I am, and if who I am is not someone's cup of tea, that is okay. We aren't for everybody, and we should not want to be for everybody. I've come to a place where I choose myself—after many years of not knowing what I was doing or who I was. I'm not only choosing me but I'm choosing a better path forward. One led by the Holy Spirit and my better judgment.

In Proverbs 2:6-10 (ESV), Solomon writes, "For the Lord gives wisdom; from his mouth come knowledge and understanding; he stores up sound wisdom for the upright; he is a shield to those who walk in integrity, guarding the paths of justice and watching over the way of his saints. Then you will understand righteousness and justice and equity, every good path; for wisdom will come into your heart, and knowledge will be pleasant to your soul." When we choose to walk with God, we are walking in wisdom and understanding. He will guide and lead us to the people and the places that are meant for us. Lean into God and His direction and He will make your paths straight.

---

1. Lamott, Anne. *Bird by Bird*. New York: Anchor Books, 1997.

Part III

Hope Even in the Unknown

Chapter Eleven

Getting on the Right Path

Walking away from a drug abuser who doesn't want to change their behavior is challenging. The love you have for that person doesn't just disappear, and it can sometimes feel like you're failing them by leaving. You want what is best for them and you think that by being there and supporting them, you are helping them realize how detrimental drugs are to their life. But sometimes that is not the case. Sometimes you need to fully walk away and let them hit rock bottom before they will realize what the drugs have done to their life and the chaos it caused to yours. There comes a time when you have to face the damage that has been done and put yourself first. It's called tough love and it's the hardest love to give, but it is the most necessary in this situation.

In the recent years of my life, hope often seemed elusive. Pinning my hope on the success of my marriage or Brent's well-being left me feeling hopeless countless times. I waited for mere breadcrumbs and pretended I was satisfied. However, as I established boundaries and initiated the process of leaving him, I held onto God more fervently. In Him, I discovered the unwavering hope that propelled me to push through and move forward.

Everything that happened with my ex-husband, and with my multiple sclerosis diagnosis, brought me to the end of myself in a way. It helped me get to the point of saying, "God, if this is where you're going to take me, because you're literally trying to show me that I just need to trust you and let things go, know that I'm there. I trust you in the unknown."

I started the process of divorcing Brent in April 2021. It's been a really hard road—very frustrating and lonely sometimes, but I know it's for the best. Over the past few years, I've learned a lot about myself. I've learned a lot about the court system. I've learned a lot about just really not caring what people think. I've learned what battles you need to put your energy into and when you need to let go of certain things that are out of your control. And most importantly, I've learned that I am more than what I went through.

The divorce process is lengthy unless both parties do not have any assets to split and no children are involved. I live in a state where they believe children benefit from having both parents involved. I agree that children need both their mother and father, but only if circumstances are safe for the children. My focus with my divorce was on proving that it was not beneficial for my children to be left alone with Brent without supervision until he proved himself a responsible, drug-free father. I had to collect and organize all the documentation I had against Brent and his drug abuse and present it to my lawyer. With God's help, I let go of trying to figure things out myself and allowed my lawyer to do her job with the evidence I had complied together.

Brent and I had a family mediation in October of 2021. Mediation typically takes three hours, but ours was done in record time. I made it clear that I was not comfortable with a 50/50 split, and unsupervised visits, and I wanted him to complete random drug testing. If he didn't agree, then I was prepared to bring our case before the judge. I wasn't interested in hearing any of his requests, so when he said no to my proposal, my lawyer and the mediator called an impasse. My lawyer informed me there were two things

I could do next. The first option was to request a hearing, but if Brent was to pass a drug test, he could be granted unsupervised visits. The second was to wait it out, set up visitations myself, and keep documentation. I chose the second option. With my children being one and two years old at the time and too young to fully communicate, I wanted to allow them time to grow before a judge made any ruling. My biggest fear was something happening to my children, and them not being able to pick up the phone to call for help. It seemed to be the wiser choice. As much as I wanted to fully end my marriage, my children's safety trumped my desire.

I communicated my schedule with Brent and set up visits in public locations. Brent always said he would take a drug test, but never once did he buy a test, and never did he provide any results. I didn't have any standing court orders to enforce this, so I proceeded with visitations that I supervised—doing as my attorney instructed, sitting back and watching his interactions with our boys. If there were any red flags, I was prepared to document them, and if they were a danger to our children, I was to remove ourselves from visitation and notify my attorney. Whenever worry tried to poke its ugly head in my doorway, I had to pray and trust that God would handle it better than I could. I reminded myself through scripture that the battle belonged to God and that the battle was already won.

I never denied Brent the opportunity to be a father. I always encouraged him to spend time with our children and made the argument on several occasions that they should always be his priority as they were mine. We often revisited this when he canceled or when he provided the minimum financially. It has been two years since family mediation, with no awaiting court date in the system. However, as my relationship with the Lord strengthened, He told me not to worry about my boys, giving me the nudge I needed to reach out to my attorney to get the ball rolling back in motion. Per my recent conversation with my attorney, my divorce will likely be finalized in February 2024, once the court reviews the information I updated. I am praying it is sooner, and I'm looking forward to this door being closed, locked, and the key being thrown into the depths of my past.

As time goes on, I'm making an effort to co-parent effectively and avoid falling into the repetitive cycle of explaining what should already be understood. I've finally accepted that I can only be my children's mother. Regardless of the challenges I encounter, I can never take on the role of being their father in his absence. It's a burden I can't carry; the shoes are not a comfortable fit for me. I've found joy in not wearing shoes that aren't meant for me. My focus is on leveraging my strengths within the role assigned to me by God. I'm content and fulfilled in just being my children's mother. When I catch myself slipping into old patterns of trying to figure everything out on my own, I raise my hands in surrender and remind myself to give it to God.

When I received the diagnosis of MS, I realized that this was something I hadn't planned for, completely out of my control. Despite my efforts to plan meticulously, everything kept falling apart around me. Multiple sclerosis taught me that when things are breaking down faster than I can piece them back together, it means I am contributing to my own destruction. It signifies that there are aspects of our lives we must let go of for something new to be created. We are the clay, and God is the potter. The more we try to impose our own design, the harder He has to remove pieces that don't belong, keeping us on the spinning wheel until we acknowledge His design is superior to ours. When I finally surrendered everything to God, I felt freedom and relief. Releasing things to Him allowed me to regain feeling in my body, and I started to see the beauty in what He was creating from my mess. Focusing on Him and taking care of myself helped me treat my body like the temple He says it is. I changed my eating habits, exercised more, and, most importantly, stopped worrying about things I couldn't control.

There is so little we can control in this life. So much of what is going to happen is unknown. That reality can either lead us to despair or lead us to God. When God asks us to surrender something or someone to Him, He is not trying to punish us, but rather lead us down the path of hope, joy, and purpose that was meant for us. There may be so much that is unknown to us, but it is known to Him, and His plan is one of prosperity and hope (see Jeremiah 29:11).

My favorite Bible verse is Proverbs 3:5-6 (NIV), "Trust in the LORD with all your heart and lean not on your own understanding; in all your ways submit to him, and he will make your paths straight." When we acknowledge Him in everything we do, He makes our paths straight. We can look straight into the unknown and know that our path is protected by the One who created us. He has a purpose for us, and when we lean into Him, we get a better understanding of that purpose, and we can walk in the path He set out for us. God wants us to be at peace with everyone if possible (Romans 12:18). My circumstance would only be possible if both parties came to an understanding and agreement.

Minister and author Gary Thomas wrote in his book *When to Walk Away*, "Sometimes to follow in the footsteps of Jesus is to walk away from others or to let them walk away from us."[1] Sometimes following the path God has for us means walking away from people or situations or jobs that do not align with where He is leading us. That process of letting go is never easy and it feels wrong at times, but it is necessary to experience the joy, purpose, and hope that is ours in Christ.

---

1. Thomas, Gary. *When to Walk Away: Finding Freedom from Toxic People*. Grand Rapids, MI: Zondervan, 2019.

Chapter Twelve
Find New Rhythms

Clearly, this wasn't the dream life I envisioned as a young girl. My circumstances have thrown several curveballs into my life plan, and I find myself on a new path that is foreign to me. But this new path is one of hope and freedom. Out of these hardships, I got my two beautiful boys and I've developed perseverance and wisdom that I wouldn't have otherwise. I've learned how to effectively recognize red flags and call them what they are.

Life isn't over when you leave or separate from the drug abuser in your life. This is just the start of your story, one part of a tale that is still unfolding. There will be more living, joy, and love for you on this path, just keep going. It can be hard to reconcile the life you wanted for yourself with the life you have. Grief is inevitable in this process, but on the other side of that grief is acceptance, joy, and strength.

God has worked miracles in my life. When I was in the beginning stages of my walk in obedience, I asked God to use what happened to me for good. I couldn't fathom going through all those hardships without a positive outcome. The idea of writing this book came to me, and as I sought confirmation, God repeatedly answered with a resounding "yes." He paved the way even when I doubted having the necessary funding or time.

The Bible is full of stories demonstrating that, despite the ugliness we may endure, beauty can emerge from our hardships. We can rise again. My own pain has enabled me to connect with those facing similar situations or who may believe that healing is out of reach. It isn't. To you, my dear friend, whoever you may be, I comprehend and share in your feelings. I understand the desire to see goodness in people, to cling to your family, and the confusion and frustration that may arise. Loss, betrayal, and pain are familiar to me. I stand with you, assuring you that things will improve. 2 Corinthians 1:3-5 (ESV) says, "Blessed be the God and Father of our Lord Jesus Christ, the Father of mercies and God of all comfort, who comforts us in all our affliction, so that we may be able to comfort those who are in any affliction, with the comfort with which we ourselves are comforted by God. For as we share abundantly in Christ's sufferings, so through Christ we share abundantly in comfort too." I firmly believe if you take a leap of faith, God will come running to you! He did it for me and He will do it for you. Your journey to healing and becoming whole is more important than your destination. I promise it's a journey worth taking!

In her book *The Gifts of Imperfection*, Brené Brown writes, "I now see how owning our story and loving ourselves through that process is the bravest thing that we will ever do."[1] I encourage you to be brave in owning your story. When we own our stories and hand all our brokenness over to the God who created us, we will begin to thrive and flourish, even in the mess and rubble and chaos of our lives. God is always, always inviting us to find rest and joy in Him. Jesus says in Matthew 11:28-30 (MSG), "Are you tired? Worn out? Burned out on religion? Come to me. Get away with me and you'll recover your life. I'll show you how to take a real rest. Walk with me and work with me—watch how I do it. Learn the unforced rhythms of grace. I won't lay anything heavy or ill-fitting on you. Keep company with me and you'll learn to live freely and lightly." If you are tired and worn out from the circumstances in your life, from being taken advantage of, from feeling like you have to do everything on your own, give your burdens to God and rest in Him. It doesn't mean that you'll never face hardship or that things will be easy, it just means you aren't alone. You have someone with you who can help you carry everything you've been trying to carry on your own for so long.

The red flags I once overlooked and clung to are now woven into my story, forming a testimony to how God's grace and hope transcend even the darkest nights and challenging seasons. I believe that God is utilizing my journey to assist others in recognizing red flags in their relationships, ultimately saving them from heartache and pain. Regardless of what you've endured or how many red flags you collected before embracing change or letting go of a relationship, understand that God will use your journey of embracing your story and loving yourself through the process to redeem, restore, and revitalize your life. When we look at our stories and think, *How did I stay so long? Why did I let them take advantage of me again? Why did I keep making the same mistakes? What is my problem?* It doesn't help us along in the healing process; instead, those thoughts stagnate us and keep us in a self-hatred that is detrimental to our very life and purpose. But when we look at our stories and think, *Wow, I endured and persisted under difficult circumstances. I did the best for what I knew at the time. I deserved to be treated better. That experience made me stronger, and I learned a lot about myself in the process,* then we are opening ourselves up to letting God use us and our stories for His glory. When we do this, we move forward; we aren't stagnant, but instead, we experience exponential growth. We begin shedding old thought processes, habits, and rhythms in favor of new and healthier ones.

After separating from Brent, I had to learn new rhythms. With my boys, with my thoughts, with my health, with my spirituality. Everything in life shifted for me, and it was difficult to find my bearings. I had a lot of healing to do, but I wasn't actively being traumatized anymore. I didn't know what was in store for me next, but I felt more confident in myself and my ability to know what was best for me and my boys. I knew I needed to find and invest in a stronger community, be more open with people in my life about how I was doing and the help I needed, and allow God to guide me to His purpose for me.

Isaiah 43:19 (NIV) says, "See, I am doing a new thing! Now it springs up; do you not perceive it? I am making a way in the wilderness and streams in the wasteland." I had been in the wilderness for so long, desperate for water, and now I feel that He has provided streams in the wasteland. He is making something beautiful out of my story.

Friend, I pray my testimony has helped you in some way. I pray you can look yourself in the mirror and see that you are unique and deserve all life has to offer. Don't allow the lies and manipulation of a drug addict to take the driver's seat in your life. Don't bypass the red flags. Don't ignore your intuition. Don't normalize chaos. Utilize the resources given to you, be courageous, and make the effort to get the help you need. You're worth it.

---

1. Brown, Brené. *The Gifts of Imperfection*. New York: Random House, 2020.

Recommendations

If you are like me and have children with an addict, it is important to recognize the severity of this issue. Pay close attention to all the red flags discussed in this book and be mindful of whom you confide in and ask for help from. Any person who enables the behavior of the addict, or anyone who tells you it's not that big of a deal, are the exact people you don't need to take advice from. Don't give your children a disadvantage by not addressing the problem you have been faced with. You are responsible for their safety and responsible for creating the barrier they need to refrain from learning these habits. Familiarize yourself with the principles God has laid out and also the organizations listed below, and look up others that may exist. Often, the organizations have support groups for family members of drug addicts. The more you know, the better you are at helping yourself and those you love.

The Bible is God's truth. It's the standard and it is filled with knowledge we are freely given to maneuver through life. God wants each of us to grow with the blueprint He has provided. The Bible speaks about everything from drunkenness to prosperity, to generational curses, and so on. Generational curses are real and seen in the bloodline of those with a drug addiction. They can be broken through prayer, fasting, and taking action to implement necessary changes in our lives. Prayer is the most powerful weapon we have been given to fight strongholds. God gives us authority in our words as stated in Proverbs 18:21 (ESV), "Death and life are in the power of the tongue and those who love it will eat its fruit." If you want to break the toxic cycle of drug abuse in your family, acknowledge it and pray about it. Declare the chain will be broken. Become the warrior in that spiritual battle. "For we do not wrestle against flesh and blood, but against the rulers, against the authorities, against the cosmic powers over this present darkness, against the spiritual forces of evil in the heavenly places" (Ephesians 6:12 ESV). Don't budge in the fight and utilize the resources around you. Get involved at a local church that is led by the Holy Spirit (refer to 1 John 4:1 to learn about the testing of the spirit) and find a support group that will pray with you and cover your family. Surround yourself in a community that is Christ-like and will come in agreement with you against these strongholds.

Several organizations aid in recovery. Although these are geared more toward helping the addict, they do offer help to family members of the addict. Alcoholics Anonymous has twelve steps and twelve traditions to help addicts overcome their drinking problem. The program relies on the accountability partner system of one addict helping another and they incorporate God-based principles. It is free and they are located nationwide. Their website is www.aa.org. A branch of Alcoholics Anonymous is Narcotics Anonymous. They too have accountability partners and follow the twelve-step principles while also integrating God's word. Their website is www.na.org. From my interaction and knowledge of these groups, they do not provide counseling or social services.

The American Addiction Centers aids in addiction treatment, medical detox, and aftercare services, and even assists with sober living facilities. They send out articles every week, which include tips and ideas to maximize a person's recovery. Their phone number is 1-888-987-1784 and they are available 24/7. I would suggest According to The American Addiction Centers, there is a possible predisposition towards addiction if a close genetic relative suffers from addiction. Environmental factors also play a significant role in addiction, including a person's culture, religion, socioeconomic factors, and lifestyle choices.

In this chapter of my life, I embraced the world of books. Turning off the television, I sought out authors who shared a Christ-centered perspective, anticipating that their words would not only nourish my spirit but also provide healing and comfort. One of the most crucial things I did was read the book of Proverbs along with *In Search of Wisdom* by Joyce Meyer. Each week I would get on a call with my aunt, and we discussed a chapter and shared insights with one another. Proverbs is considered the book of wisdom in the Bible and when I was going through my storm, I needed all the wisdom I could get. I meditated over scripture that stuck out to me and did my best to apply its principles to my daily life. The verses in this book are still ones I refer back to when I feel lost. I also kept Romans 12:2 in the forefront of my mind so I wouldn't fall back into the old thoughts I fought so diligently to detach from.

I know that everyone's healing journey is different, but I would be selfish if I didn't share with you what worked for me. God is ultimately responsible for my healing and the more I submitted myself to Him, the more He paved the way for me to obtain knowledge and the resources to get help, heal, and thrive.

I sincerely pray that the information provided serves as the catalyst you require to overcome your challenges and empowers you to rise above all that you have endured.

God bless you!

Acknowledgements

First and foremost, I want to thank God for being with me through it all. I've always known God is real and always present, but never experienced how truly powerful He is until I fully surrendered myself to Him. God, thank you for being my rock. Thank you for hearing my cries and answering my prayers. Thank you for wiping my tears and comforting me. Thank you for lifting me when I couldn't get up. Thank you for sending an abundance of help when I asked. Thank you for your love, grace, peace, mercy, protection, and favor. Thank you for showing me that you were already walking ahead of me when I decided to stop walking down a road that was not meant for me to go down. Thank you for your wisdom. Thank you for my purpose. Thank you for keeping your promises. Thank you for never disappointing me. Lord, I owe everything that I am and everything that I have to You. You have been so good to me, and I thank you for it all. Nothing is impossible for You. I love you with all of me.

Thank you to my parents, Ma and Padre, for everything you have done and sacrificed to help me get through my storm. I am so blessed to have your support, encouragement, and love, even when I felt I was an embarrassment to you. Thank you for the push to not turn back. Thank you for helping with the boys on countless occasions. Thank you for doing all you could do to make my circumstances bearable. I could never repay you, but

I hope to be all that you are to me, to my children. I love you both.

To my siblings, close friends, and other family members (you know who you are), a million thanks for all you have done. Thank you for standing in my corner and loving me through my flaws, hardships, and growth. I will forever be grateful to each one of you for the outpour of love I have received. I truly am blessed to have you all in my life. I love you guys.

About the Author

Jessica Lewis's story is a powerful testament to resilience and the transformative power of faith. By sharing her journey of being married to a drug addict, Jessica not only sheds light on the struggles she faced but also aims to empower others who may be dealing with similar challenges.

As a licensed athletic trainer with experience in various settings, Jessica brings a unique perspective to her ministry work. Her background in health and sports, coupled with her newfound focus on ministry, allows her to approach empowerment from a holistic standpoint.

The debut of her book, *Don't Bypass Red Flags*, suggests a candid and insightful exploration of recognizing warning signs and navigating the complexities of relationships with individuals struggling with addiction. Through her writing, Jessica aims to guide individuals in recognizing their self-worth, establishing healthy boundaries, and finding strength in moments of despair by relying on the promises of God.

Jessica lives in Central Florida with her two sons. Her life is a blend of her passion for ministry, love for literature, and commitment to family. Her interests include reading self-help and poetry books, writing, visiting the beach, and spending quality time with loved ones.

www.ingramcontent.com/pod-product-compliance
Lightning Source LLC
Chambersburg PA
CBHW020408130626
46549CB00006B/2478